Contra.

18. Medius — Tomkins's — Cantoris

Forty yeares long was I grieued w^th this generation & sayd: It is a people that doe err in their hearts.

Glory be to ye Father & to ye Son & to ye holy Ghost as it was in ye beginning & is now & euer shall be.

world w^th out end. A - - - men. We knowledge thee to be ye Lord all ye earth doth

worship ye Father everlasting. To ye all angels cry aloud ye heauens & all ye powers therein

Holy Holy Holy Lord God of Sabaoth Lord God of Sabaoth Heauen & earth are full of ye Ma^ie

of ye glory. The goodly fellowship of ye Prophets praise ye. The holy Church throughout

all ye world doeth knowledge ye. Thine honou^ble true & only Son. Thou art ye King of glory

O Christ. O Christ. Thou art ye euerlasting Son of God. When ye tooke upon ye to deliuer man

thou didst not abhorre ye virgins wombe. Thou didst ouercome ye sharpe sting of death. When thou

ye thou shalt come to be ye Judge. Wh^ch thou hast redeemed w^th thy precious blood be pleased

them to be numbred w^th ye Saints. O Lord saue ye people

ye name. Vouchsafe O Lord to keep us ye day

T0057087

A Study

of the

BING-GOSTLING PART BOOKS

in the

Library of York Minster

together with

a Systematic Catalogue

by

Watkins Shaw
Honorary Librarian
St Michael's College, Tenbury
1948-85

Published for the

Oxford University Press
Walton Street Oxford OX2 6D

© The Royal School of Church Music, 1986

Transferred 1994 to
Oxford University Press

C O N T E N T S


| | | Page |
|---|---|---|
| Introduction | | 3 |
| References | | 19 |
| End-note: Bing as Lay Vicar of Westminster Abbey | | 21 |
| The Catalogue | | 23 |
| Medius Decani | | 24 |
| Contratenor Decani | | 35 |
| Tenor Decani | | 45 |
| Bassus Decani | | 54 |
| Medius Cantoris | | 63 |
| Contratenor Cantoris | | 70 |
| Tenor Cantoris | | 77 |
| Bassus Cantoris | | 84 |
| Index to the Catalogue | | 89 |
| Appendix I | The Westminster Abbey-Tucker-Bing connection | 107 |
| Appendix II | The St Paul's Cathedral-Bing-Gostling connection | 112 |
| Appendix III | Chapel Royal part-books of 'Anthems with Symphonies in the hand of William Tucker | 114 |

# LIST OF PLATES

Frontispiece and between pp. 22 & 23


I The hand (A) of Stephen Bing. York Medius Cantoris book, f. 14v (p.18)

II The hand (B) of Stephen Bing. York Bassus Cantoris book, f. 76v (p.144)

III Inscription inside front cover York Bassus Cantoris book

IV Heading and signatures, Accounts of the College of Minor Canons of St Paul's Cathedral, 1660-61

V The hand of John Gostling. York Bassus Decani book, f.69v (p.132)

# INTRODUCTION

The Library of the Dean and Chapter of York Minster stands possessed of eight volumes of manuscript forming a set, uniform in size (30.5 x 19.5 cms more or less) containing a repertory of English cathedral music of the period c1570-1695. Respectively (though with some irregularity) the volumes furnish the separate voice parts for Medius, Contratenor, Tenor, and Bassus, each for both sides of a choir, decani and cantoris. While they have all been subject to repair and cropping, each book substantially retains its late 17th-century leather binding. The present collective library reference is M.1.S.

They have for some considerable time been known as the 'Gostling' part-books because they formed part of the collection of William Gostling (c1695-1777), Minor Canon of Canterbury Cathedral, whose signature and book-plate is found in each.[1] As will presently appear, however, there is an earlier and closer Gostling connection. William Gostling's significant collection ('musicae reconditae eximiaeque locuples') was sold by Langford, as traced by A. Hyatt King, Some British Collectors of Music (Cambridge, 1963), on 26 and 27 May 1777 (not by Flackton, as stated in the Dictionary of National Biography), and in the unique surviving copy of the sale catalogue, now Hirsch IV, 1003 in the Music Room of the British Library (Reference Division), the following description of Lot 82 undoubtedly refers to these volumes:

> A complete Choir set of Anthems and Services, by the more early Composers for the Church, in 8 vol. written by Sub-Dean Gostling.

The reference to 'Sub-Dean Gostling' will be elucidated below.

It is not known who acquired them in 1777 nor how the books reached York. They were listed in the York Minster Catalogue of 1850 with the remark 'These are part Books for a Choir and most beautifully written'.[2] The first scholars of any importance to consult them were the editors of Tudor Church Music (1922-29) who, however, in saying they were 'Begun about the middle of the seventeenth century' dated them earlier than can be justified.

By whom, when, and for what purpose were these books compiled, and what is their significance?

To answer the first question we must rely on the testimony of handwriting, of which three types are exhibited, shown respectively in Plates I, II, and V. Inside the front cover of the Bassus Cantoris book is a brief memorandum (Plate III) relating to 28 April 1679 made by one 'Steph. Bing', and this clearly identifies him as the scribe of hand II (Plate II). Readers of biographies of Purcell [3] will recognise the name Stephen Bing as that of one who copied music for Westminster Abbey in the 1670's, and enquiry reveals the following entry in the Abbey unofficial register under the date 26 November 1681:

> Mr Steven Bing dyed and buried the 1st day of December at Canterbury.[4]

Pursuing this, the burial of 'Mr. Stephen Bing' on that date may be traced at St George's Church, Canterbury. In his Will[5] dated 12 February 1680/81 he asked to be buried there near his father and mother, a fairly certain hint that he may have been baptised in that parish; and so it proves. 'Stephan, son of Stephan Binge' was baptised at St George's on 20 September 1610.[6] His Will describes him as 'Clerk one of the Minor Canons of St Paul's London', and in sum these clues enable us to piece his career together as follows.

He was a chorister of Canterbury Cathedral, first named as such in the accounting year ending Michaelmas 1618 and last mentioned in the year ending 1624 when his name, though entered in the fair copy accounts, was struck through. It seems that he did not proceed to sing as a man in Canterbury Cathedral choir in any of the various capacities of melody man, substitute, lay clerk, or minor canon,[7] and we lose trace of him for some 17 years. But he evidently acquired Holy Orders, and in the year ending Midsummer 1642 his name occurs for the first time at St Paul's Cathedral when, in the Accounts of the College of Minor Canons,[8] he signed for his dividend that year. He was still there when the last dividend before the Interregnum was distributed at Midsummer 1649.

A glimpse of his interests is provided by a contemporary pencil memorandum in these accounts for 1646-47: 'Lent Mr Binge ye 23° of July 1647 Morlyes Introduction' (i.e., A Plaine and Easie Introduction to Practicall Musicke by Thomas Morley, 1597). But his tenure at St Paul's was interrupted by the cessation of Prayer Book worship and the abolition of capitular bodies. Apparently he stayed in London, and he figures in John Playford's list, given in A Musicall Banquet, 1651, of 'excellent and able Masters' then available to give tuition, he being named 'For Voyce and Viole'. His association with viol music is supported by his MS transcription of 3-part 'Fantazies & Aires' by Jenkins, Locke, and Young[9] of which more will presently be said (see p.8 ). Meanwhile, the Trustees for the Maintenance of Ministers (a Commonwealth body) allotted him pittances of £4 and £2 in 1655 and 1657 respectively.[10]

He was on the spot immediately St Paul's Cathedral began to function again upon the Restoration in 1660 when he and a certain Henry Smith were the only two surviving Minor Canons in priest's orders (the third survivor,

Randolph Jewett, was only a deacon). It was arranged that he should exchange his existing patent as a simple Minor Canon for a new one as Minor Canon and Senior Cardinal, and he was admitted as such on 14 May 1661.[11] For the first two years after the Restoration he was also Warden of the College of Minor Canons, and the accounts of that body for the years ending Midsummer 1661 and 1662 are carefully written by him.

Once more, however, his work was to be interrupted, this time by the destruction of St Paul's Cathedral in the Fire of London, 1666. Though the choir ceased to function properly for some 30 years, the Minor Canons, being in occupation of a freehold, still qualified for their annual dividend, and their accounts show that Bing collected this in 1671 to 1681 inclusive (years ending at Midsummer) and he was allowed it posthumously for 1682. But the men of the choir were permitted to seek employment elsewhere for the time being, and on 21 March 1666/7 Bing was appointed a Senior Vicar Choral (i.e., a vicar in Holy Orders) at Lincoln Cathedral.[12] There, so far as is known, he remained until an opportunity occurred to return to London and he was admitted as a Lay Vicar of Westminster Abbey on 1 April 1672 when he signed the Precentor's Book.[13] The Abbey accounts[14] give us glimpses of his activity in copying music there, surviving vestiges of which are referred to in Appendix I *infra*.

Year ending Michaelmas

| | |
|---|---|
| 1673 | To Stephen Bing for ruled papyr for a set of Quirebooks . . . £2 |
| 1676 | To Mr Bing for Books for the Church for ye last year 1675 then omitted . . . xxxiil ls vid |
| 1679 | To Mr Bing for writing 29 sheets and 23 staves . . . xxxviijs |

He remained in his dual capacity of Minor Canon of St Paul's and Lay Vicar of Westminster Abbey until his death in November 1681.[15]

Thus far we have followed the clue of Plate III and its identification of the scribe of Plate II. What of the hand shown in Plate I, that of the earliest entries in the book? This, too, despite its differences, is that of Bing, as revealed by comparison with the Accounts of the College of Minor Canons of St Paul's Cathedral which Stephen Bing wrote out for 1661 and 1662 (see Plate IV; any remote possibility that there were two men of that name at St Paul's either concurrently or successively is quite ruled out on the evidence of the muniments).

The overall impression on comparing the two styles of hand is of greater cursiveness in Plates I and IV as against more angular stiffness in Plates II and III. More detailed comparison shows that <u>in general</u> the minuscules g, w, and y, for example, are distinguished thus: in the hand of Plates I and IV the 'g' is more likely to have a sloping, simply looped descender, the 'w' more likely to be rounded in formation, the 'y' almost always formed like a 'u' together with a simple downward stroke for descender, while the ascender of a 'd' may be either vertical or backward looping. By contrast, the hand of Plates II and III tends to have a 'g' with a tightly curled descender, a 'w' formed more like a double 'v', and a 'y' with a sharp angle between two separate strokes, of which the descender slopes markedly backward and under, while the ascender of a 'd' is almost without exception stiffly upright.

But it will also be observed that even within one and the same document the descender of the 'g' can vary, notably in Bing's own name, so that the hand of Plate IV reveals this now with a 'g' as in that of Plates II and

III, now as in that of Plate I. Yet, examining his signatures in various years in the St Paul's accounts we find sometimes one, sometimes the other (in the Precentor's Book of Westminster Abbey we find the 'g' with the sloping, simply looped descender, the only signature of his to survive at the Abbey). And although many pages of the York books are differentiated from each other in the two styles of Plates I and II respectively, others show signs of instability in this respect. Thus, in the Tenor Cantoris book, Farrant's 'High' Service, in the style of Plate I, shows besides the 'g' characteristic of that style, a form of this minuscule associated with Plates II and III; while in Rogers's Service in G the Creed has 'y' in the style of Plate I, but Magnificat shows that of Plate II. Furthermore, though the Viol Fantasies which, as already mentioned, Bing transcribed have only a minimum of verbal text, they too exhibit sometimes the more flowing cursive of Plate I, and sometimes the stiffer manner of Plate II, e.g. (Treble book, f.1) 'Mr Joh: Jenkins's Fansies of 3 Parts' compared with (Bass book, f.19) 'Mr Math: Locks Fansies & Aires of 3 Parts'.

All in all, therefore, despite a first general impression of separate scribes, it must be concluded that Plates I and II simply represent different styles of one and the same hand, and that everything in the York books except items in the hand of Plate V was written by Stephen Bing.

The hand of Plate V is easily identified as that of John Gostling, and can be authenticated by reference to his signatures in the Accounts of the College of Minor Canons of St Paul's Cathedral, his endorsement on the fly-leaf of Egerton MS 2959 in the Reference Division of the British Library, and, most freely, in the Parish Register, now in Canterbury Cathedral Library, which he maintained as Vicar of Littlebourne. John Gostling is a better-known figure than Bing, and so his career can be more succinctly described.

He is likely to be the John Gostling who was admitted to St John's College, Cambridge in October 1668. Having been ordained at what would seem to be almost the earliest canonical age, he was admitted Minor Canon of Canterbury Cathedral in November 1675, probably after a year's probation, and appointed Vicar of Littlebourne, Kent at the same time. Described as 'a base from Canterbury, Master of Arts', he was sworn a Gentleman of the Chapel Royal on 28 February 1678/9,and on 23 January 1681/2 (hard on Bing's death) he began a probationary year as a Minor Canon of St Paul's Cathedral, being later admitted Subdean there on 15 January 1689/90 - which last appointment explains the expression recorded above from the W. Gostling Sale Catalogue of 1777.[16] He retained these various posts as well as his living at Littlebourne until his death at an advanced age in 1733.

It is the fact of John Gostling's handwriting in the York books which gives them a stronger Gostling connection than that simply of their possession by William Gostling. They must have passed into John Gostling's hands on Bing's death, doubtless because of the St Paul's Cathedral link between the two men, and they naturally passed to his son William on his own death.

The elder Gostling is known as a transcriber of music apart from the York books. A large album in score, now in the Humanities Research Center of the University of Texas, Austin, USA, is a personal collection of anthems based on the Chapel Royal repertory of 1670-1705.[17] A small MS in the Euing Collection, University of Glasgow (R.d.47) consists of secular songs for bass, of interest to him as a renowned basso profundo for whom Purcell's

'They that go down to the sea in ships' was conceived. A book of organ parts to anthems which he copied c1705-10 is MU.MS 669 in the Fitzwilliam Museum, Cambridge, and a stray bass voice part of Blow's 'I beheld, and lo! a great multitude' is now Tenbury MS 1225. There are also three pages (50-52) in his writing (Blow, 'Sing we merrily'; Wise, 'O praise God in his holiness') in a bass part-book, E10-20, at Canterbury Cathedral, and a good deal of his work can be seen in surviving part-books at St Paul's Cathedral (see Appendix II *infra*). But his largest legacy of church music in part-books is found in Tenbury MSS 797-803 and 1176-82 deposited in the Bodleian Library, Oxford, about which something will be said presently.

If, as his own memorandum indicates, Bing was working on these books in April 1679, then he may well have done so almost up to his death in November 1681, which gives the latest date for the transcripts in his hand. When did he begin the books? The distinction between 'Mr Rogers' and 'Dr Rogers' within the space of some 15 leaves early on in each book may suggest that he started not long before Rogers acquired his doctorate in July 1669 (unless, transcribing later than that, he mechanically copied 'Mr Rogers' from the document in front of him). That he was not writing much before 1670 is indicated by his description of Thomas Tudway as organist of King's College, Cambridge in the section devoted to verse anthems, an appointment Tudway took up in the autumn of 1670. The same impression is given by a sectional heading in the earlier Plate I hand of Bing, 'A Collection of...Anthems...made at Lincoln... (16)68, 69, & 70' (Medius Decani, f.83). As Bing was at Westminster Abbey from 1672 reliance may be placed on his distinction between 'Mr Blow' and 'Dr Blow', and this shows that nearly all of the works by Blow in his hand were transcribed before December 1677. These considerations lead one to conclude that he began the books about

1668-70 while at Lincoln, brought them with him on his return to London, and copied the most considerable substance in them between 1672 and 1678, but may have continued his transcriptions until shortly before his death.

Gostling's additions are obviously later than 1681, and he was still using the books after William Turner took his doctorate in 1696 and late enough to copy Blow's 'My God, my God', composed 6 September 1697. But because 'Dr Turner' and this anthem by Blow come at almost the latest point of Gostling's entries, and he gives nothing by Clarke or Croft, he probably abandoned these books somewhat before 1700.

As to the function of the books, it is obvious that they were not designed for, and are incapable of use in, practical performance from choir stalls. Even when they are most carefully written, the stave ruling and the space between the staves is too close for that purpose. Choir books of this period have more generous staves permitting larger note heads, and more space between staves making for ease in reading the words. When, on a preliminary leaf of the Tenor Decani book, Bing wrote 'A Book of Services and Anthems for a Quire' he was referring to contents, not format. Furthermore, in a true set of choir books even a four-part composition would be copied twice to provide for both 'decani' and 'cantoris'. In the York books Bing begins conscientiously by doing this, but presently realises it is unnecessary for his purpose so long as each of the four parts is represented once, as in Blow's 'O how amiable'. In a five-part work (say MAATB), for choir book purposes M, T, and B would each be entered in both sets of books together with A(I) in the Decani book and A(II) in the Cantoris book, but it is enough for Bing that he writes William Mundy's five-part Service in all four Decani books and uses the Cantoris books only for the additional alto part. Byrd's six-part 'Sing joyfully' is correspondingly treated, and there are other examples. When copying Gibbons's 'Hosanna to the Son of David' Bing went so far as to write the unison Tenor part in both books, but then, realising the position at that point, did not trouble to duplicate the unison Bass part. A further consideration against use in choir stalls is that at times his script becomes very cramped, and his text contains various annotations and some supplementary slips of inserted paper, making reading difficult. As for Gostling's contributions, his script is frankly informal, and by the time the books reached him they were becoming so full that in some instances (e.g., Purcell's 'O God, thou art my God', a five-part work) he could only find room for the two Tenor parts by putting them both into the Cantoris book. Finally, for practical use they would have required much better indexing.

The fact is that these books are the file copies of a professional transcriber, from which on request he could draw the large fair copies needed for a choir in performance. It happens that this state of affairs is precisely confirmed by Tenbury MSS 797-803 and 1176-82, both written by Gostling. The former set consists of seven books out of an original eight, as at York, and they exhibit the same sort of narrow stave ruling and minimum space between the staves; the latter set is generous in both respects with carefully formed notes and clear words. And the significant point is that the repertory in the larger set (1176-82) is very substantially drawn from the contents of the smaller set (797-803) thus demonstrating the existence of a file set belonging to the copyist and a choir set drawn therefrom, presumably as a commission. That both sets are now in the same library is probably fortuitous.[18]

The contents transcribed by Bing may be considered from more than one point of view. But first there is the minor point that they testify to free-lance copying of parts for cathedral (etc.) choirs. One would have supposed that, in the normal way, a copyist would, as a set task, draw out parts for a given choir (as Bing himself did for Westminster Abbey and St Paul's Cathedral) from specified compositions supplied to him for the purpose, and it is by no means easy to see what market there could have been for the work of the owners of such file copies as these. But here appears to be evidence that such a possibility was envisaged. Copies for personal use would surely have been in score. What we do not know is whether, when copying for the Abbey or St Paul's, Bing transcribed from these books, or whether he assembled them as a result of doing that work.

However that may be, as the period of their compilation can be defined, broadly speaking, within c1670-c1680, it might be hoped that they would help towards the dating of works by composers then active, Blow, Purcell, Turner, and Wise. And so they might, if no other evidence were forthcoming. But a list of music copied into the books of the Chapel Royal between 1670 and 1676[19] firmly provides narrower limits than Bing's transcripts, and the amount of other music transcribed elsewhere by William Tucker (see Appendix I *infra*) necessarily testifies to its having been composed before his death in 1679. For John Blow these books tell us that 'God be merciful' and 'I will cry unto thee' probably pre-date December 1677; they are the prime testimony to a date earlier than December 1681 for Purcell's 'Give sentence with me', 'O praise the Lord, all ye heathen', and 'Save me, O God', as also for Wise's Services in D minor and E major and his 'Blessed is the man'. It is possible that they may help a little also with some works by William Turner.

Next, Bing's choice of works for his collection suggests some points of interest in relation both to those composed before the Civil War and Commonwealth, and to those written after the Restoration of Charles II in 1660.

So far as the earlier group is concerned he evidently assumed that his potential clients would not have access to Barnard's First Book of Selected Church Musick (1641), even though, as we know, a stock of that publication survived the Interregnum; for among a considerable number of Barnard's items Bing included all the Full Anthems except Byrd's 'O God, whom our offences', Sheppard's 'Haste thee, O God', and Tallis's 'Wipe away my sins'. But it may be significant of the taste for which he was catering that he chose only three of the ten Verse Anthems published by Barnard. As to Services, of Barnard's 15 Bing covers six, none of them a verse Service.

Yet, on the other hand, Bing gives Services from this period not published by Barnard, as follows: Amner (2), Batten, J.Farrant, R.Farrant, Patrick, Portman, and T. Tomkins. Further, he copied anthems not found in Barnard's publication thus: Batten (13), Bull (2), Byrd (1), Dering (1), O.Gibbons (6), W.Lawes (2), Morley (1), Portman (2), Ramsey (2), J.Tomkins (1), T.Tomkins (5), Ward (3), R. or W.White (1). In addition, there are some less well-known figures like Ed(ward) Smith and Thomas Wilkinson.

Traces of the repertory of pre-Civil War music in use at Westminster Abbey after the Restoration survive in fragments (significantly, in Bing's hand) of a contemporary choir book, Tenor Decani '5', discussed in Appendix I *infra*. Here we find four Services and 18 Anthems composed before *c*1640, all save one Service and one Anthem being in the York books also. Bearing in mind that the testimony of this single Westminster Abbey book is fragmentary only, it may well be that the correspondence between the books now at York and the Abbey repertory of this class of music in the 1670's was in fact greater. If so, then to the extent that we now lack evidence of the nature of that repertory it may well be supplied by the York books.

If it is clear that there is some correspondence between Bing's books and the Abbey repertory in this regard, want of comprehensive evidence makes its impossible to say whether, or to what extent, it may have been shared by the Chapel Royal in the 1670's. But, moving to music of the later period, taking in that of senior men such as Child, C.Gibbons, Locke, Rogers, and Tucker as well as the rising young men of that decade - Aldrich, Blow, Humfrey, Turner, Wise, and the still youthful Henry Purcell - we find that the central and substantial core of Bing's repertory is closely related to that of both Westminster Abbey and the Chapel Royal at this time, ignoring, not unexpectedly, the special category of 'anthems with symphonies' that was distinctive of the Chapel Royal alone. Testimony to this is directly to hand, firstly in two part-books (Alto Cantoris 'No 1A' and Tenor Cantoris 'No 4') surviving at Westminster Abbey which contains items copied between c1670 and the death of William Tucker in 1679 (see Appendix I infra). Secondly, this is supported by the list of music copied into the books of the Chapel Royal 1670-76 (see footnote 19). Bing gives all the Services named there and among the Anthems he includes all those by Blow, C.Gibbons, Humfrey,[20] Tucker, and Turner, and nearly all of those by Child and Wise, a substantial total of 49 anthems in common.

Beyond that central correspondence, however, Bing's York part-books display some individual characteristics. His representation of Christopher Gibbons and Turner is somewhat stronger than at the Chapel and Abbey so far as present knowledge goes, and he takes cognisance of some lesser composers like Henry Hall and William King as well as of the odd figure of Silas Taylor. He also seems exceptional in choosing as many as six works by George Jeffreys. His inclusion of fairly numerous anthems by Hecht and Cutts is not only a reminder of his own connection with Lincoln Cathedral, of which Hecht became organist in c1663 and Cutts a Junior Vicar Choral in 1664, but of the existence of provincial composers unrecognised in the metropolis, so helping us to see the period in better perspective.[21]

Finally there is the matter of the textual value of Bing's transcripts. The lack of an organ part is obviously a serious gap in the complete text of a verse anthem.[22] Otherwise two elements are in play here, the nature of the sources available to a scribe and the extent of his reliability as a faithful copyist.

About the first of these it is impossible to generalise, as it will vary with different parts of Bing's repertory. Separate judgments concerning individual works or groups of works must be made by specialist textual scholars in relation to whatever other sources of ascertainable authority are available. A few superficial points suggest themselves, however. Where pre-Civil War music is involved there may well be a prima facie case to consider whether a scribe working c1670 may not have been relying on Barnard's 1641 publication. Only careful sifting could settle that, so possibly separating scribal slips from readings of independent authority. But it may be significant that in copying at least one group of works included by Barnard in 1641 Bing preserves exactly the same sequence of works.

Barnard's publication, however, includes by no means all the pre-Civil War music in these part-books, and it is an open question whence Bing derived his text of the remainder.

In the 20th century editors have been able to draw, inter alia, on pre-Civil War MSS at Peterhouse, Cambridge and on MSS of similar date and of early post-Restoration date at Durham Cathedral, none of them available to Bing. Even if - a pure guess - he had access to Barnard's manuscript books (RCM MSS 1045-51) these would by no means have supplied all he needed. Whatever the reliability or provenance of his transcripts, it would seem that they represent a line of transmission independent of other early post-Restoration sources of these works.

In the particular instance of Thomas Tomkins, Bing plainly implies that he had access to a source other than Musica Deo Sacra (1668), and that must be the publication he means when he annotates his transcripts by reference to what he calls 'ye printed books'. How far Nathaniel Tomkins's publication of his father's work in 1668 is regarded as being of the purest essence, I do not know; but it is certainly interesting, and perhaps significant, to find traces of its circulation independent of that publication.

Reaching music closely contemporary with the date of his copying, one cannot but suppose that Bing obtained text of Blow, Humfrey, Turner, Wise, and, later, Purcell from sources close to the composer; and it is evident that he took some opportunity, at least, to compare his work with other authoritative transcripts. The fact remains, of course, that where (as with Blow, for instance) we have manuscripts in the composer's own hand, such copies as these of Bing are of far less significance (I do not say no significance at all). But otherwise, at face value, for this school of composers they are of no less significance so far as they go than those in, for example, MU.MS 117 in the Fitzwilliam Museum, which also represent one remove from a prime source. And it is by the single thread of

Bing's testimony that one work, 'Give sentence with me', by Henry Purcell hangs.

On the question of his reliability in copying, he was sufficiently interested in what he was doing to make textual annotations here and there, and the neatness of his earlier entries makes a very good impression. But there are uncomfortable signs of lack of order, and there is a disturbing number of incomplete texts. Even his heading about anthems composed at Lincoln, 1668-70 in the Medius Decani book is not repeated in the other books. In general, while his transcripts certainly merit attention and must be taken into account when no over-riding other authority is available, it may be suggested that perhaps he should be regarded circumspectly, with the possibility of error, not only alternative readings worth collation, in mind.

ACKNOWLEDGMENTS

I am most grateful to the Librarian and other officers of York Minster Library for agreeable and friendly facilities when consulting the manuscripts in their care, and for permission to reproduce Plate I, II, III, and V. I similarly acknowledge the kindness of the Librarians of Westminster Abbey and St Paul's Cathedral, and the permission of the Custos of the College of Minor Canons of St Paul's to reproduce Plate IV.

REFERENCES

1. His book-plate embodies a coat-of-arms, 'Gules, a chevron ermine between 3 crescents argent', executed in trick. This seems to have been made up and assumed by approximation to two slightly different achievements of arms associated with the names Gos(s)elyn, Gosling, Gooseling and Gosselin.

2. Information kindly supplied by Mr David Griffiths.

3. W.H.Cummings, Purcell (1881); J.A.Westrup, Purcell (1937 and subsequent revisions).

4. J.L.Chester, The Marriage, Baptismal, and Burial Registers of the ... Abbey of St Peter, Westminster (1876).

5. Public Record Office PROB 11/368/179 (olim 179 North).

6. See The Registers of St George the Martyr, Canterbury, ed. J.M.Cowper (Canterbury 1891). One 'Steven Bing' whom we take to be the father, was buried there on 31 August 1632, and 'Mary Binge', a widow and probably the mother was buried on 3 February 1637/8. Other entries appear to show that our subject was the only son and second child of five.

7. Canterbury Cathedral, Fair copy accounts Nos 26-47, 1617-42 (with gaps); Bound papers of accounts, 1576-1642 (with gaps).

8. Guildhall Library, London, St Paul's Cathedral Muniments, F.B.6.

9. Guildhall Library, London, Gresham College Collection, G Mus 469-71.

10. A.G.Matthews, Walker Revised, 1948.

11. Guildhall Library, London, St Paul's Cathedral Muniments, Minute Book 1660-64, F.C.1; Muniment Book 1660-95, W.C.45.

12. Guildhall Library, London, St Paul's Cathedral Muniments, Minute Book F.C.2, 22 November 1666; Lincolnshire County Record Office, Lincoln Cathedral Chapter Acts A.3.11, f. 254.

13. W(estminster) A(bbey) M(uniments) 61228A, f. 130

14. W.A.M. 33700, 33710, 33714.

15. Sir Jack Westrup strenuously opposed the idea that Bing combined these two capacities and considered that there were two men of the same name. The matter is discussed in an End-note on p.21 .

16. For all these details, see J. & J.A.Venn, Alumni Cantabrigienses, Part 1, (Cambridge, 1922); The Old Cheque Book of the Chapel Royal, ed. E.F.Rimbault, (1872); Guildhall Library, London, St Paul's Cathedral Muniment Book 1660-95 (W.C.45), ff. 175, 219v. With regard to the post of Sub-dean it should be said, lest this be misunderstood, that it does not mean he was an important functionary as deputy to the Dean. Among the minor canons there were offices which, as it were, mirrored in parvo those of the

dignitaries - for the Precentor there was the Succentor; for the Treasurer there was the Sacrist; and to complete the pattern though (unlike the others) without corresponding duties, for the Dean there was the Sub-dean.

17. For a discussion of this document, see my review in Music & Letters, vol. 61 (1980), pp. 487-90, of the published facsimile.

18. The repertory in 797-803, the 'file set', suggests that Gostling moved over from the York set to this c1700. The much earlier and famous set of part-books compiled by John Barnard before the Civil War (now in the Royal College of Music,(MSS 1045-51) also constitute a transcriber's file, not choir books, in just the same way, though they were also used as printer's copy for The First Book of Selected Church Musick (1641). Barnard, the compiler of these books c1622-38, was a Minor Canon of St Paul's Cathedral, and from 1642 Bing was one of his junior colleagues. Barnard does not appear to have survived the Interregnum. Is it fanciful to wonder whether RCM MSS 1045-51 passed from Barnard to Bing as a result of this association, and then, along with Bing's other books now at York, to John Gostling by a like association, with the result that both sets now carry the bookplate of William Gostling?

19. H.C.de Lafontaine, The King's Musick (London, 1909), pp. 305-7.

20. At the mention of Humfrey's name the reader may have hesitated after the recent references to anthems with symphonies. Though Humfrey's works were indeed performed in the Chapel Royal with symphonies, the fact is that the York part-books taken together with those at Westminster Abbey make it clear that even at this early date they were used elsewhere without them. Some loss is involved in their omission, but these symphonies are completely detachable without causing the structure to collapse, except, to some degree in 'By the waters of Babylon', and here, in spite of the strictures that have been passed upon it, the adaptation for organ only as given in a copy in the hand of no less a person than Purcell (British Library (Reference Division), Add. MS 30932, f.52) must have been that employed for this anthem outside the Chapel Royal in conjunction with voice parts such as Bing transmits.

21. Thus also Tenbury MS 1442 (deposited in the Bodleian Library), of similar date, which includes among a general repertory works by Silver, Holmes, and Jewett, composers of local repute in Winchester and Salisbury.

22. Bing's part-books are not alone in this. Neither the printed nor the manuscript sets of Barnard have any associated organ book, and indeed there are indications generally that the compilation of organ parts was a job left to the organists, independent of the copying sets of voice parts. The organ books forming part of Tenbury MSS 1176-82 seem to be exceptional in this respect.

End-note. Bing as Lay Vicar of Westminster Abbey

Two objections might be raised to the identification of Stephen (Steven) Bing, Lay Vicar of Westminster Abbey, with Stephen Bing, Minor Canon of St Paul's Cathedral.

First, it might be said that a minor canon, being a clergyman, would not hold a post as a lay singingman. There is no substance in this. No legal barrier exists, and at that time the distinction between a minor canon (or vicar-choral in Holy Orders) and a lay singingman was far less than now, all minor canons taking their full part as choir singers and not confining themselves to intoning the priest's part of the services. There is, moreover, a known parallel. Randolph Jewett, likewise Minor Canon of St Paul's at the time of the Great Fire, availed himself of permission to take up work elsewhere and went to Winchester Cathedral to take up the post of organist, for which Holy Orders were not required. There he stayed until his death, and, like Bing, he continued to qualify for his dividend as Minor Canon of St Paul's. A lay vicar received less stipend than a minor canon, it is true; but Bing, still secure in his St Paul's dividend, was well placed to ignore that for the sake of an opportunity to get back to London from Lincoln.

Second, there is the curious fact that the Accounts of Westminster Abbey show Bing as a lay vicar for the years ending Michaelmas 1682 and 1683, that is to say after his death. Inspection of these Accounts in general easily disposes of this difficulty.

They listed the officers in order of seniority. In the year following the death of, say, the third in seniority his name would be omitted, all the others would move up by one line, and a new name added at the bottom of the list. But it was sufficient for the clerk to account for the right number of stipends, and he was not invariably watchful about names. A case in point crystallises this. William Tucker, Minor Canon of Westminster, died in February 1678/9, but in the Accounts ending at Michaelmas 1679 the clerk left his name undisturbed. Then, at Michaelmas 1680 and 1681 his name, which had been third in seniority out of four, is omitted, and that of Thomas Linacre comes in as fourth in seniority. So far, so good: but at Michaelmas 1682 Tucker's name reappears in its old position and Linacre is not mentioned.

In view of the entry of the death of a 'Steven Bing' in the unofficial Register of the Abbey, the identity of the signature in the Precentor's Book there with specimens at St Paul's Cathedral, one has no difficulty in supposing that the clerk of the 1682 and 1683 Accounts was not watchful enough to omit Bing's name when copying his list (maybe with last year's in front of him) and to bring in that of his successor.

Bass9: Vers Anthems Cantoris

W: Gostling.

Munday be^t 28. Ap: 79. about 1 of y^e clock in y^e day time was M^r Aurdens will
was opend in y^e pnce of y^e Principle of Cliffords Inn & me Steph: Bing

61.

32

The Accompt of Stephen Bing late Warden of ye Colledge of ye 12 Minor Canons of St Pauls Cathedrall Church London of all Receipts of rents he hath received or ought to have received or belonging to ye said Colledge As also the Expenses he hath expended for & upon ye Colledge aforesd from ye Feast of St John the Baptist 1660 (exclusive) at or about wch time it pleased Almighty God ye Gracious King Charles the 2d to restore ye Church to its rights & revenews) unto ye same Feast of St John 1661 inclusive.

Sum expended more than rate to

Stephen Bing

Henry Smyth.

Let every thing that hath breath praise the Lord praise the Lord
Let every thing that hath breath praise the Lord
Let every thing that hath breath praise the Lord.
Alleluia alleluia alleluia alleluia
Alleluia, alleluia alleluia
Alleluia alleluia alleluia alleluia
Vers: 32
O clap yor Hands
Vers. 24
He shall chuse out an heritage for us
Vers. 3. vo.
God is gone up
God is gone up
merry noise
sing praises unto the Lord
sing praises unto
For God is King of
all the Earth
sing ye praises
sing ye praises
Alleluiah alleluiah alleluiah alleluia
Alleluia alleluiah alleluia alleluia alle
lu=ia
Sec for the alleluia Chorus
Vers.
The Lord shall make
people offer their free will of=fering
Vers.

# C A T A L O G U E

## Explanatory notes

In the lists which follow, names of composers are given exactly as found in the manuscripts, except that Christian names have been added here and there to avoid confusion, and abbreviated Christian names have been expanded. Both these types of addition are in italic. But a few Christian names - 'Ben', 'Thos', 'Will/Wm/Willm' - have been left so, as not having the oddity of some others. Where no name is attached to any item in the manuscripts, this has been supplied in one of two ways: (a) in brackets, from the Index to the book in question; (b) in italic, from some other source of identification.

The titles of Services are also given exactly as found, but with occasional clarification (in italic), as for example 'in E minor'.

The first words of Anthems have been modernised, chiefly in accordance with the Book of Common Prayer.

In the Index, modern standardised forms of names ('Byrd' - reluctantly - for 'Bird') and designations of Services are used.

The components of Services are indicated by numerals, thus:

(1) Venite, exultemus Domino
(2) Te Deum, laudamus
(3) Bendicite, omnia opera
(4) Benedictus Dominus
(5) Jubilate Deo
(6) Responses to Commandments
(7) Creed
(8) Magnificat
(9) Cantate Domino
(10) Nunc Dimittis
(11) Deus Misereatur

The sign * distinguishes items in the hand of John Gostling.

(1) Medius Decani


| | |
|---|---|
| Inside front cover: Signature 'W.Gostling' and bookplate<br>Fly leaf | |
| A Table of all ye Services contained in ys Book | 1 |
| f.1v blank | |
| A table of all ye Anthems contained in ys Book | 2-4 |
| f.4v blank | |
| Mr Tallis Short Service (1,2,4,6,7,8,10) | 5-6 |
| Mr Strogers Short Service (1,2,4,6,7,8,10) | 6v-8 |
| Mr Birds Short Service (1,2,4,6,7,8,10) | 8-9v |
| Mr Thos Tomkins Short Service (1,2,4,6,7,8) | 10-11v |
| Mr Bevins Short Service (1,2,4,6,7,8,10) | 11v-14 |
| The Nunc Dimittis of Mr Thomas Tomkins's<br>Service in C fa ut<br>(This disturbs the continuity of Bevins's Service) | 12-12v |
| Mr Orlando Gibbons Short Service (1,2,4,6,7,8,10) | 14-15v |
| Mr Albertus Brynes Short Service (2,5,6,7,8,10) | 15v-16v |
| Mr Ben Rogers Short Sharp Service<br>D Sharp (2,5,6,7,8,10) | 16v-18 |
| Behold now, praise the Lord (Benjamin Rogers)<br>at the close of this item: 'The end of<br>Mr Rogers short sharp service' | 18 |
| Dr Childs Service in D sol re sharp (2,5,6,7,8,10) | 18v-20v |
| Dr Childes Service in E minor (2,5,6,7,8,10) | 20v-22 |
| Dr Childes Service in F (2,5,6,7,9,11) | 23-24 |
| Mr Richard Farrants high Service (2,4,6,7,8,10) | 24-26 |
| Mr Portmans Service (2,4,6,7,8,10) | 26-27 |
| Mr Thomas Tomkins Service<br>in D sol re (2,5,6,7,8,10) | 27v-28 |
| Mr William Mundy's Service of 5 Parts<br>2 Contratenors (1,2,4,6,7,8,10) | 28v-31 |
| Dr Rogers's Service in Gamut (2,5,6,7,8,10) | 31v-32 |
| Mr Pellam Humfreys Service in<br>E minor (2,5,6,7,8,10) | 32v-33 |
| Mr John Farrants Short Service (2,5,8,10) | 33v-34 |
| Mr Battens Short Service (2,5,6,7,8,10) | 34v-35 |
| Dr Rogers's Service in E la mi (2,5,6,7,8,10) | 35v-36v |
| Mr Blows Short Service in G (2,5,8,10) | 36v-37 |
| Mr Patricks Service (2,4,8,10) | 37-38 |

| | | |
|---|---|---|
| Dr Childs Benedicite Service (3,5,6,7,8,10) | | 38-38bis v |
| *Out of the deep | Henry Aldrich | 38bis v |
| 'Full Anthems' (heading) | | 38v |
| Almighty God, we beseech thee, give ear | Thos Heardson | 38v |
| O Lord, give thy holy spirit | Thomas Tallis | 38v |
| O God, be merciful unto us | Nicholas Strogers | 38v-39 |
| Call to remembrance | Mr Richard Farrant | 39 |
| Keep, we beseech thee, O good Lord | Thos Heardson | 39 |
| Hide not thou thy face | Richard Farrant | 39v |
| I will exalt thee (with 2nd part, 'Sing unto the Lord') | Dr Tye | 39v-40 |
| O Lord, the maker of all thing | Mr William Mundy | 40 |
| O Lord, the world's Saviour | (William Mundy) | 40-40v |
| Teach me thy way | Edmund Hooper | 40v |
| Almighty and everlasting God | Orlando Gibbons | 40v |
| O praise the Lord, all ye heathen | Adrian Batten | 40v-41 |
| Deliver us, O Lord (with 2nd part,'Blessed be the Lord God') | Orlando Gibbons | 41 |
| Hide not thou thy face | Adrian Batten | 41 |
| Lord, we beseech thee give ear | Adrian Batten | 41v |
| Haste thee, O God (with 2nd part,'But let all those that seek thee') | Adrian Batten | 41v |
| When the Lord turned again the captivity | Adrian Batten | 41v |
| O God, whose neverfailing providence | Andrew Hecht | 42 |
| Blow out the trumpet | (Martin Peersons) | 42 |
| Zadok the priest | Henry Lawes | 42 |
| I give you a new commandment | John Cutts | 42v |
| Sing, O daughter of Zion | Wilm Turner | 42v |
| Mr Willm Tuckers Benedicite Service (3,5,6,7,8,10) | | 42v-43 |
| Mr Willm Tuckers Short Service (2,5,8,10) | | 44-44v |
| O give thanks (Ps. 105) | Wilm Tucker | 44v |
| 'Anthems for 4 voyces' (heading) | | 45 |
| Praise the Lord, O my soul (Ps. 103) | Dr Child | 45 |

| | | |
|---|---|---|
| My soul truly waiteth | Adrian Batten | 45 |
| Deliver us, O Lord | Adrian Batten | 45 |
| O sing joyfully | Adrian Batten | 45v |
| O clap your hands | Dr Child | 45v |
| O Lord, grant the king a long life | Dr Child | 45v-46 |
| If the Lord himself | Dr Child | 46 |
| O pray for the peace of Jerusalem | Dr Willm Child | 46-46v |
| Mr John Amners Service called Caesar's (2,5,6,7,8,10) | | 46v-48 |
| O come hither, and hearken | John Amner | 48 |
| Mr John Amners Service of 4 parts (2,4,6,7,8,10) | | 48v-50 |
| Mr Patricks Commandments & Creed | | 50 |
| Mr John Blows Service in A re (2,5,6,7,9,11) | | 50v-51v |
| Mr Michael Wises Morning & Evening Service in D Minor (2,5,8,10) | | 51v-52 |
| Dr Childs Service in A re (i.e. A minor) (2,5,6,7,8,10) | | 52-53 |
| Dr Childs flatt Service in E la mi(2,5,6,7,8,10) | | 53-53v |
| Dr Childs Te Deum to his Benedicite, or his Service in Gamut (2,9,11) | | 54-54v |
| Mr Blows Benedicite Service or in E minor (3,5,6,7,9,11) | | 54v-56v |
| The Commandments & Creed to Mr Blows Service in G | | 56v |
| The Commandments and Creed to Mr Wises Service in D minor | | 56v-57 |
| Mr Wises Commandments & Creed in E sharp (i.e., E major) | | 57 |
| Dr Blows Te Deum in E minor | | 57-57v |
| Mr John Ferabosco's Evening Service for Verses in D sol re sharp (8,10) | | 57v-58 |
| Mr Aldridg's Service in E la mi (3,5,6,7,8,10) | | 58-58v |
| & his Service in Gamut (2,5,6,7,8,10) | | 58v-59 |
| A Second Creed (in triple time with Resp. to Commandments) in G of Dr Blows | | 59v |
| Mr Daniel Henstridgs Service with verses (2,5,6,7,8,10) | | 59v-60v |
| *Mr Purcel's Te Deum etc. in B flat (2,5,6,7,8,10) | | 60v-61v |
| 'Anthems of 4 Parts' (heading) | | 62 |
| Teach me,O Lord | Dr Rogers | 62 |

| | | |
|---|---|---|
| Let my complaint come before thee | Adrian Batten | 62-62v |
| O Lord God of hosts | Willm Turner | 62 |
| The Lord hear thee | John Blow | 62v |
| O God, the king of glory | Henry Pursel | 62v-63 |
| Dr Blow's Te Deum to his Benedicite Service in E la mi | | 63-63v |
| f.64/64v blank | | |
| 'Full Anthems of 5 Parts' (heading) | | 65 |
| With all our hearts | Thos Tallis | 65 |
| Blessed be thy name, O God | Thos Tallis | 65 |
| O thou God, Almighty Father | Edmund Hooper | 65 |
| I call and cry | Thos Tallis | 65-65v |
| O Lord, I bow the knees of my heart | William Mundy | 65 |
| Prevent us, O Lord | Willm Bird | 65v-66 |
| Behold, it is Christ | Edmund Hooper | 66 |
| O Lord, make thy servant Charles | Willm Bird | 66 |
| I lift my heart to thee | Dr Tye | 66v |
| O Lord, turn thy wrath (with 2nd part, 'Bow thine ear') | Willm Bird | 66v-67 |
| O give thanks | Dr Giles | 67 |
| O come let us sing unto the Lord | Robert Ramsey | 67v |
| Why art thou so full of heaviness? | Thomas Wilkinson | 67v |
| O Jerusalem, thou that killest the prophets | Thomas Wilkinson | 67v-68 |
| Almighty God, the fountain of all wisdom | Thomas Tomkins | 68 |
| Save me, O God (Ps. 54) | (William Birds) | 68v |
| The Lord bless us | Willm White | 68v |
| We beseech thee, Almighty God | Adrian Batten | 69 |
| O give thanks unto the Lord (Ps. 105) | Willm Tucker | 69 |
| O clap your hands | William Tucker | 69v |
| I will sing unto the Lord | Henry Pursell | 69v-70 |
| O Lord, I have loved the habitation | Thos Tomkins | 70 |

| | | |
|---|---|---|
| O God, wherefore art thou absent? | Will Turner (recte John Blow) | 70 |
| The king shall rejoice | John Tomkins | 70-70v |
| Save me, O God (Ps. 69) | Mr Blow | 70v |
| Save me, O God (Ps. 54) | Henry Pursell | 70v-71 |
| *O give thanks ...and his mercy | Dr Aldrige | 71 |
| *Have pity upon me, o ye my friends | Mr Wise | 71-71v |
| *I beheld, and lo! a great multitude | Dr Rogers | 71v-72 |
| *Blessed is the man (Ps.1) | (Mr Sargenson) | 72 |
| *O praise the Lord (Ps. 135) | Dr Child | 72v |
| *Service in A minor (8,10) | Dr Rogers | 72v-73 |
| *I waited patiently | John Blow | 73-74 |
| 'Anthems for 6 & for more Parts' (heading) | | 74v |
| O praise God in his holiness | Willm White | 74v |
| *O praise the Lord (Ps. 135) | (Dr Child) | 74v |
| Deliver me from mine enemies | Robt Parsons | 75 |
| Sing joyfully | Willm Bird | 75 |
| *O sing unto the Lord (Ps. 98) (ending only) | William Child | 75 |
| Hosanna to the Son of David | Orlando Gibbons | 75v |
| Lift up your heads | Orlando Gibbons | 75v-76 |
| O Clap your hands | Adrian Batten | 76 |
| Lord, who shall dwell in thy tabernacle? | Adrian Batten | 76 |
| God is our hope and strength (a 8) | Mr John Blow | 76v |
| O clap your hands ('Dr Hethers Commencement Song') (with 2nd part,'God is gone up') | Mr Orlando Gibbons | 76v-77 |
| Inclina Domine | (Mr Ramsys) | 77-77v |
| *Prepare ye the way ('2nd Treble in T.C.book') | Mr Wise | 77v |
| *O sing unto the Lord (Ps. 98) (ending on f.75) | Dr Child | 78 |
| *O praise God in his holiness | (Mr Wise) | 78-78v |
| *O clap your hands ('2nd Treble in T.C.book') | Dr Rogers | 78v |

| | | |
|---|---|---|
| *The Lord said unto my Lord ('2nd Treble in T.C.book') | Mr Wise | 79 |
| *Thy way, O God, is holy | Mr Purcell | 79 |
| Blessed be the Lord my strength | Henry Purcell | 79v |
| Hear, O heavens | Mr Pellam Humfrys | 79v |
| O how amiable are thy dwellings | John Blow | 79v |
| Lord, thou hast been our refuge | William Turner | 79v |
| Behold, God is my salvation | Thomas Tudway | 79v-80 |
| Lord, teach us to number our days | Mr Pelham Humfrys | 80 |
| O give thanks (Ps. 118) | Mr Pellham Humfrys | 80-81 |
| Like as the hart | Mr Pellham Humfry | 80v |
| O Lord, thou hast searched me out | Mr John Blow | 80v-81 |
| *Behold now, praise the Lord | (Dr Blows) | 81 |
| *Hear my prayer, O Lord (Ps.102) | Mr Turner | 81 |
| *I will sing a new song | Mr Wise | 81v |
| *I will alway give thanks | Pelham Humfrey, John Blow, William Turner | 81v |
| *O give thanks (Ps.106) | Henry Purcell | 82 |
| *Teach me, O Lord | Dr Christopher Gibbons | 82v |
| 'A Collection of such Anthems for verses as have bin made at Lincoln in ye years 68, 69 & 70' (heading) | | 83 |
| O praise the Lord (Ps.147) | Willm Turner | 83 |
| Hear my crying, O God | Andreas Hecht | 83 |
| By the waters of Babylon | John Cutts | 83 |
| Praise the Lord, ye servants | Andreas Hecht | 83-83v |
| Comfort ye, my people | Willm Tucker | 83v |
| Sing unto the Lord, O ye kingdoms | Willm Turner | 83v |
| The earth is the Lord's | Willm Turner | 83v-84 |
| This is the day | Willm Turner | 84 |
| O be joyful in God | Willm Turner | 84 |
| Blessed is the man (Ps.1) | Andreas Hecht | 84 |
| Praise the Lord, O my soul (Ps.103) | Andreas Hecht | 84v |

| | | |
|---|---|---|
| Lord, who shall dwell in thy tabernacle? | Andreas Hecht | 84v |
| My days are gone | John Cutts | 84v-85 |
| O praise the Lord, ye angels | John Cutts | 85 |
| Haste thee, O God | Andreas Hecht | 85 |
| Behold, how good and joyful a thing | Willm Turner | 85 |
| O sing unto the Lord (Ps.98) | John Cutts | 85v |
| Sing, O daughter of Zion | Willm Turner | 85v |
| O praise the Lord (Ps.147) | Willm Turner | 86 |
| Behold, God is my salvation | William Turner | 86 |
| By the waters of Babylon | Willm Turner | 86v |
| O Lord, thou hast searched me out | John Blow | 86v |
| Sing we merrily | John Blow | 86v-87 |
| Holy, holy, holy | Adrian Batten | 87 |
| Unto thee, O Lord, will I lift up | Richard Dering | 87-87v |
| By the waters of Babylon | Mr Pellam Humfrey | 87v |
| Not unto us (Note in Index:'As it is in Mr Tucker's Books') | Mr Lock | 87v |
| Let God arise | Willm Lawes | 87v |
| Blow up the trumpet | Henry Purcell | 87v-88 |
| I will praise the Lord | John Ward | 88v |
| Out of the deep | Adrian Batten | 88v |
| 'Anthems for Verses' (heading) | | 90 |
| Almighty God, who by the leading of a star | Dr Bull | 90 |
| In thee, O Lord, put I my trust | Dr Bull | 90-90v |
| Behold, thou hast made my days | Orlando Gibbons | 90v |
| Blessed are all they | Orlando Gibbons | 90v-91 |
| Behold, I bring you glad tidings | Orlando Gibbons | 91 |
| Glorious and powerful God | Orlando Gibbons | 91-91v |
| If ye be risen again with Christ | Orlando Gibbons | 91v |
| Out of the deep | Thomas Morley | 91v-92 |
| How long wilt thou forget me? | Thomas Morley | 92 |

| | | |
|---|---|---|
| How long wilt thou forget me? | Albertus Bryne | 92-92v |
| How long wilt thou forget me? | Dr Christopher Gibbons | 92v-93 |
| My beloved spake(Note: 'Thus in ye printed book') | Thos Tomkins | 93 |
| Thou are my king, O God | Thos Tomkins | 93-93v |
| O Lord, make thy servant Charles | Willm Cranford | 93v |
| My song shall be of mercy | Henry Lawes | 93v |
| Now that the Lord hath re-advanced the crown | William King | 93v-94 |
| Let all the world in every corner sing | Henry Loosemore | 94 |
| O how amiable are thy dwellings | Mr Loe (Edward Lowe) | 94-94v |
| O how happy a thing it is | Adrian Batten | 94v |
| Bow down thine ear | John Ward | 94v |
| I will magnify thee | (John Wards) | 94v-95 |
| O Lord our governor | Adrian Batten | 95 |
| Unto thee, O Lord, do I lift up | Will Tucker | 95-95v |
| Above the stars my saviour dwells | Dr Christopher Gibbons | 95v-96 |
| Behold, I bring you glad tidings | Ben Rogers | 96-96v |
| O give thanks (Ps.107) | Ben Rogers | 96v |
| O that mine eyes would melt | George Loosemore | 96v-97 |
| Hear my prayer, O Lord, and let thine ear | Thomas Wilkinson | 97-97v |
| Preserve me, O Lord (concluded on f.98v) | Thos Wilkinson | 97v-98 |
| Let God arise | (John Wards) | 98 |
| The Lord is my light | Willm Lawes | 98-98v |
| Hear my crying, O God | Andreas Hecht | 98v-100 |
| I will give thanks (Ps.138) | John Cutts | 100 |
| Comfort ye, my people | Wilm Tucker | 100-100v |
| O come hither and hearken | (John Cutts) | 100v |
| Praise the Lord, ye servants | Willm Tucker | 100v-101 |

| | | |
|---|---|---|
| Lord, who shall dwell in thy tabernacle | Mr Portmans | 100v-101 |
| Lord, how long wilt thou be angry? | Willm Tucker | 101 |
| Lord, who shall dwell in thy tabernacle? (concluded) | Richard Portman | 101v |
| O Lord, thou hast searched me out | Adrian Batten | 101v |
| Hear my prayer, O God | (Adrian Battens) | 101v-102 |
| I heard a voice from heaven saying, Allelujah | Albertus Bryne | 102-102v |
| Blessed is the man (Psalm 1) | Michael Wise | 102v |
| Lord, what is man? | Willm Turner | 102v |
| Lord, let me know mine end | (Matthew Locks) | 102v-103 |
| Turn thy face from my sins | Mathew Lock | 103-103v |
| O give thanks (Ps.107) | Willm Tucker | 103v |
| Wherewithal shall a young man cleanse? | Willm Tucker | 104 |
| Lord, how are they increased | John Blow | 104 |
| Behold how good and joyful a thing | John Blow | 104v |
| Awake up my glory | Michael Wise | 104v |
| God standeth in the congregation | Henry Hall | 104v-105 |
| I will cry unto thee, O God | John Blow | 105 |
| How are the mighty fallen | Michael Wise | 105-105v |
| Turn thee unto me | John Blow | 105v-106 |
| Rejoice in the Lord, O ye righteous | Pelham Humfreys | 106 |
| I will magnify thee | Will Tucker | 106 |
| I was glad | Will Tucker | 106-106v |
| Christ being raised from the dead | John Blow | 106v-107 |
| By the waters of Babylon | Michael Wise | 107 |
| Christ being raised from the dead | John Blow | 107-107v |
| Blessed is he that considereth the poor | Michael Wise | 107v |
| The Lord said unto my Lord | Dr Christopher Gibbons | 107v-108 |

| | | |
|---|---|---|
| O praise the Lord, all ye heathen | Dr Christopher Gibbons | 108-108v |
| Rejoice in the Lord, O ye righteous | Richard Portman | 108v |
| Not unto us | Matthew Lock | 108v |
| My God, my God, look upon me ('Organist of Kings Colledge in Cambridge') | Thos Tudway | 109 |
| This is the day | Willm Tucker | 109-109v |
| O Lord our governor | Henry Pursell | 109v-110 |
| Have mercy upon me | Pellham Humfrys | 110 |
| O Lord, I have sinned | Mr Blows | 110-110v |
| Christ being raised | Mr John Blow | 110v |
| God be merciful unto us | Dr Christopher Gibbons | 110v-111 |
| Let God arise | Henry Pursel | 111 |
| Behold, how good and joyful a thing | Dr Childs | 111 |
| Lord, I am not high minded | Dr Christopher Gibbons's | 111v |
| Let God arise | Dr Child | 111v |
| Sing unto the Lord, O ye saints | Dr Christopher Gibbons | 112 |
| Out of the deep | Willm Grigory | 112 |
| God be merciful unto us | John Blow | 112v |
| Thou art my king, O God | Dr Child | 112v |
| O God, thou hast cast us out | Willm Grigory | 113 |
| Awake, put on thy strength | Michael Wise | 113 |
| Mr Pursel's chorus to his Anthem O praise the Lord, all ye heathen | | 113 |
| *I was glad | Mr Pursel | 113 |
| *Try me, O God | Dr Turner | 113v |
| *O God, to whom vengeance belongeth | Anonimous J.B. (recte John Blow?) | 113v |
| *When the Son of Man shall come | Dr Blow | 113v |
| *God is our hope and strength | (Dr Aldrich) | 114 |
| *Hide not thou thy face | R.Farrant, adapted by Henry Aldrich | 114-114v |

| | |
|---|---|
| *Give sentence with me | (Dr Aldrich) based on 114v O.Gibbons,'Almighty and everlasting God' |

Inside back cover: Eight Psalm Tunes (Single Chants):

| | |
|---|---|
| William Child | F |
| John Blow | E minor |
| 'T.P.' | G minor (Zimmerman, D.33 |
| 'E.P. | D minor (Zimmerman, Z.123) |
| William Turner | A |
| | D |
| | B minor |
| Pelham Humfrey | C (the 'Grand Chant') |

(2) Contratenor Decani

Inside front cover: 'W.Gostling' and bookplate

Fly-leaf, containing (i) some indecipherable pencil note;
(ii) in Bing's hand:
Begotten of his see if ye crotchet be in D & E
or in C & D in ye Contratenor of Childs service
in D sharp.


A Table of all ye Services contained in ys Book 1

f.1v blank

A Table of all ye Anthems contained in ys Book 2-4

f.4v blank

Mr Tallis's Short Service (1,2,4,6,7,8,10) 5-6v

Mr Strogers his Short Service (1,2,4,6,7,8,10) 6v-8v

Mr Birds Short Service (1,2,4,6,7,8,10) 8v-10

Mr Thos Tomkins Short Service in C (1,2,4,6,7,8,10) 10v-12

Mr Bevins Short Service (1,2,4,6,7,8,10) 12-13v

Mr Orlando Gibbons Short Service (1,2,4,6,7,8,10) 13v-15

Mr Brynes Short Service (2,5,6,7,8,10) 15v-16v

Mr Benjamin Rogers Short Service (2,5,6,7,8,10) 16v-17v

Behold now, praise the Lord Benjamin Rogers 17v

Dr Childes Sharp Service in D (2,5,6,7,8,10) 17v-19v

Dr Childes Service in E minor (2,5,6,7,8,10) 19v-20v

Dr Childs Service in F (2,5,6,7,9,11) 20v-22
(note at end: 'Examined by ye King's Books')

Mr Richard Farrant High Service (2,4,6,7,8,10) 22-23

Mr Portmans Service (2,4,6,7,8,10) 23v-24v

Mr Thomas Tomkins Service in D minor (2,5,6,7,8,10) 24v-26v

Mr William Mundy's Service of 5 Parts
2 Contratenors (1,2,4,6,7,8,10) 26v-28v

Dr Rogers's Service in Gamut (2,5,6,7,8,10) 29-30

Mr Pellam Humphrys Service in E la mi (2,5,6,7,8,10) 30-30v

Mr John Farrants Short Service (2,5,6,7,8,10) 31-31v

Mr Adrian Batten's Short Service (2,5,6,7,8,10) 31v-32

Dr Rogers's Service in E la mi (2,5,6,7,8,10) 32v-33

Mr John Blows Short Service in G (2,5,8,10) 33v-34

Mr Patricks Service (2,4,8,10) 34-34v

Dr Childs Benedicite Service (3,5,6,7,8,10) 35-36

Mr Tuckers Benedicite Service (3,5,6,7,8,10) 36-37

Mr John Blow's Benedicite Service (3,5,6,7,9,11) 37-38v

| | | |
|---|---|---|
| Mr John Amners Caesars Service of 5 parts (2,5,6,7,8,10) | | 38v-40 |
| O come hither, and hearken ('The Anthem to the Service') | John Amner | 40 |
| Mr Patricks Kyrie & Creed | | 40v |
| Mr Blows Service in A re (2,5,6,7,9,11) | | 40v-41v |
| Mr Michael Wises Morning & Evening Service in D minor (2,5,8,10) | | 41v |
| Dr Childs Service in A re (i.e.A minor) (2,5,6,7,8,10) | | 42-43 |
| Dr Childs Flatt Service in E (2,5,6,7,8,10) | | 43-43v |
| Dr Childs Te Deum to his Benedicite Service | | 43v-44 |
| Dr Childs Evening Service in Gamut (9,11) | | 44-44v |
| The Commandments & Creed to Mr Blows Service in G | | 44v-45 |
| Dr Child's Service in E la mi sharp (i.e. E minor) as it is on Cantoris Side (2,5,6,7,8,10) | | 45-45v |
| Mr Wises Commandments & Creed in E la mi Sharp (i.e., E major) | | 46 |
| Dr Blows Te Deum to his Benedicite Service (incomplete) | | 46v |
| Mr Alldrigs Service in E la mi (3,5,6,7,8,10) | | 46v-47v |
| Mr Ferabosco's Evening Service for Verses (8,10) | | 47v |
| Mr Aldrigs Service in Gamut (2,5,6,7,8,10) | | 47v-48v |
| Dr Blows 2nd Creed in G (triple time) (6,7) | | 48v |
| *Mr Purcells Service in B flat (2,4,6,7,8,10) | | 48v-49v |
| f.50 blank | | |
| 'Full Anthems of 4 Parts' (heading) | | 51 |
| Almighty God, we beseech thee | Thos Heardson | 51 |
| O Lord, give thy holy spirit | Thos Tallis | 51 |
| O God, be merciful | Nicholas Strogers | 51 |
| Call to remembrance | Richard Farrant | 51v |
| Keep, we beseech thee, O good Lord | Mr Heardson | 51v |
| Hide not thou thy face | Richard Farrant | 51v |
| I will exalt thee (with 2nd part,'Sing unto the Lord') | Dr Tye | 51v-52 |
| O Lord, the maker of all thing | Willm Mundy | 52 |
| O Lord, the world's saviour | Willm Mundy | 52v |
| Teach me thy way | Edmund Hooper | 52v |
| Almighty and everlasting God | Orlando Gibbons | 52v |

| | | |
|---|---|---|
| O praise the Lord, all ye heathen | Adrian Batten | 53 |
| Deliver us, O Lord (with 2nd part,'Blessed be the Lord God of Israel') | Orlando Gibbons | 53 |
| Hide not thou thy face | Adrian Batten | 53 |
| Lord, we beseech thee give ear | Adrian Batten | 53 |
| Haste thee, O God (with 2nd part, 'But let all those that seek thee') | Adrian Batten | 53v |
| When the Lord turned again the captivity | Adrian Batten | 53v |
| O God, whose never failing providence | Andrew Hecht | 53v |
| Blow out the trumpet | Martin Pearson | 54 |
| Zadok the priest | Henry Laws | 54 |
| Sing, O daughter of Zion | Willm Turner | 54 |
| I give you a new commandment | John Cutts | 54v |
| Behold, how good and joyful a thing | Wm Turner | 54v |
| Deliver us, O Lord God | (Adrian Battens) | 54v |
| My soul truly waiteth | Adrian Batten | 54v-55 |
| Praise the Lord, O my soul (Ps.103) | Dr Child | 55 |
| O sing joyfully | (Mr Battens) | 55 |
| O clap your hands | Dr Child | 55v |
| O Lord, grant the king a long life | Dr Child | 55v |
| If the Lord himself | Dr Child | 55v |
| O pray for the peace of Jerusalem | Dr Willm Child | 56 |
| Teach me, O God | Dr Rogers | 56-56v |
| O God, the king of glory | Henry Pursel | 56v |
| Let my complaint | Adrian Batten | 56v |
| The Lord hear thee | John Blow | 57 |
| *O give thanks... and his mercy | Dr Aldridge | 57 |
| *Mr Wises Creed in D minor | | 57-57v |
| *O clap your hands | Dr Rogers | 57v |
| *The Lord said unto my Lord | Michael Wise | 57v-58 |
| *O clap your hands (Medius Decani) | (Dr Rogers) | 58 |

| | | |
|---|---|---|
| *Thy way, O God, is holy | (Mr Purcell) | 58-59 |
| *O give thanks (ps.106) | Henry Purcell | 59-60 |
| *Teach me, O Lord | Dr Christopher Gibbons | 60 |
| *Behold, I bring you glad tidings ('For Christmas Day') | Henry Purcell | 60v-61 |
| *Out of the deep | Dr Aldrich | 61 |
| *O praise the Lord (Ps.135) | Dr Child | 61v-62 |
| *I waited patiently | Dr Blow | 62 |
| *Try me, O God | (Dr Turner) | 62-62v |
| *O be joyful in God (Decani and Cantoris) | Mr Dr Blow | 62v-64v |
| *Thy word is a lantern (very imperfect) | Henry Purcell | 64v-65 |
| ff.65v and 66 blank | | |
| 'Full Anthems of 5 Parts' (heading) | | 67 |
| With all our hearts | Thos Tallis | 67 |
| Blessed be thy name | Thos Tallis | 67 |
| O thou God, Almighty Father | Edmund Hooper | 67 |
| O Lord, I bow the knees of my heart | Willm Mundy | 67-67v |
| I call and cry | Thos Tallis | 67v |
| Prevent us, O Lord | Willm Bird | 67v-68 |
| Behold, it is Christ | Edmund Hooper | 68 |
| O Lord, make thy servant Charles | Willm Bird | 68 |
| I lift my heart to thee | Dr Tye | 68-68v |
| O Lord, turn thy wrath (with 2nd part,'Bow thine ear') | Willm Bird | 68v-69 |
| O Give thanks | Dr Giles | 69 |
| O come let us sing unto the Lord | Robert Ramsey | 69-69v |
| Why art thou so full of heaviness? | Tho Wilkinson | 69v |
| O Jerusalem, thou that killest the prophets | Thos Wilkinson | 69v |
| Almighty God, the fountain of all wisdom | Thos Tomkins | 70 |
| Save me, O God (Ps.54) | Willm Bird | 70 |

| | | |
|---|---|---|
| We beseech thee, Almighty God | Adrian Batten | 70v |
| Lord, who shall dwell in thy tabernacle? | Adrian Batten | 70v |
| Hear my prayer, O God | Adrian Batten | 70v-71 |
| O give thanks (Ps.105) | Willm Tucker | 71 |
| O clap your hands | Adrian Batten | 71-71v |
| The Lord bless us and keep us ('This Anthem is to be put on Cantoris side') | Willm White | 71v |
| Turn thy face from my sins | Matthew Lock | 71v-72 |
| I will sing unto the Lord | Henry Pursell | 72 |
| O clap your hands | Willm Tucker | 72-72v |
| O Lord God of hosts | Willm Turner | 72v |
| O Lord, I have loved the habitation | Thos Tomkins | 73 |
| Save me, O God (Ps.54) | Henry Pursel | 73 |
| *Hear my prayer, O Lord (Ps.102) | Mr Turner | 73 |
| *Praise the Lord, O my soul (Ps.146) | Mr Loosmore | 73v |
| *Have pity upon me, O ye my friends | Mr Wise | 73v |
| *Hear my prayer, O Lord (Ps.102) | Mr Turner | 74 |
| Mr Robert Ramsy's Commencement Song of 8 Parts Inclina Domine | | 74v |
| Dr Hethers Commencement Song composed by Mr Orlando Gibbons O clap your hands | | 75 |
| 'Anthems of 6 or more Parts' (heading) | | 75v |
| Sing joyfully unto God | Will Bird | 75v |
| Deliver me from mine enemies | Robert Parsons | 75v |
| Hosanna to the Son of David | Orlando Gibbons | 76 |
| Lift up your heads (note:'Batten, Lord who shall dwell & O clap your hands are among ye 5 parts') | Orlando Gibbons | 76 |
| The king shall rejoice | Joh Tomkins | 76v |
| O God, wherefore art thou absent? | Mr Blow | 76v |
| God is our hope and strength (a 8) | Mr Blow | 76v-77 |
| Save me, O God (Ps.69) | Mr Blow | 77 |

| | | |
|---|---|---|
| O praise God in his holiness | Willm White | 77 |
| Holy, holy, holy | Adrian Batten | 77v |
| Unto thee, O Lord | Richard Deering | 77v |
| Behold, God is my salvation | Mr Tedway | 78 |
| I will praise the Lord (completion at foot of f.77v) | (Mr Wards) | 78 |
| Praise the Lord ye servants | Andrew Hecht | 78v |
| Lord, I am not high minded | Dr Christopher Gibbons | 78v |
| 'Anthems for Verses' (heading) | | 79 |
| Almighty God, who by the leading of a star | Dr Bull | 79 |
| In thee, O Lord, put I my trust | Dr Bull | 79 |
| Behold, thou hast made my days | Orlando Gibbons | 79v |
| Blessed are all they | Orlando Gibbons | 79v |
| Behold, I bring you glad tidings | Orlando Gibbons | 79v-80 |
| Glorious and powerful God | Orlando Gibbons | 80-80v |
| If ye be risen again with Christ | Orlando Gibbons | 80v |
| Out of the deep | Thos Morley | 80v-81 |
| How long wilt thou forget me? | Thos Morley | 81 |
| O Lord, let me know mine end | Thos Tomkins | 81-81v |
| Let God arise | John Ward | 81v-82 |
| Thou art my King, O God | Thos Tomkins | 82 |
| O Lord, make thy servant Charles | Willm Cranford | 82-82v |
| I heard a voice from heaven saying, Allelujah | Albertus Bryne | 82v |
| O praise God in his holiness | Edward Smith | 82v-83 |
| Hear my prayer, O Lord, and let thine ear | Thos Wilkinson | 83 |
| My song shall be of mercy | Henry Laws | 83 |
| Now that the Lord hath readvanced the crown | William King | 83-83v |

| | | |
|---|---|---|
| Let all the world in every corner sing | Henry Loosmore | 83v |
| How long wilt thou forget me? | Albertus Bryne | 83v-84 |
| My beloved spake | Thos Tomkins | 84 |
| O how happy a thing it is | Adrian Batten | 84-84v |
| Christ rising again | Adrian Batten | 84v |
| Bow down thine ear | (Adrian Batten) (recte Ward) | 84v |
| I will magnify thee (attrib.'Mr Ward' in Index) | John Cutts | 85 |
| O Lord our governor | Adrian Batten | 85 |
| Unto thee, O Lord, do I lift up | Willm Tucker | 85-85v |
| How long wilt thou forget me? | Dr Christopher Gibbons | 85v |
| Above the stars the saviour dwells | Dr Christopher Gibbons | 85v-86 |
| Behold, I bring you glad tidings | Ben Rogers | 86 |
| The earth is the Lord's | William Turner | 86 |
| By the waters of Babylon | John Cutts | 86-86v |
| Blessed is the man (Ps.1) | Andreas Hecht | 86v-87 |
| Behold, God is my salvation | Willm Turner | 87-87v |
| My days are gone | John Cutts | 87v |
| O praise the Lord, ye angels | John Cutts | 87v-88 |
| O sing unto the Lord (Ps.98) | John Cutts | 88-88v |
| O be joyful in God | Willm Turner | 88v-89 |
| The earth is the Lord's | Willm Turner | 89-89v |
| This is the day | Willm Turner | 89v-90 |
| Sing unto the Lord, O ye kingdoms | Willm Turner | 90 |
| Haste thee, O God | Andreas Hecht | 90-90v |
| Hear my crying, O God | Andreas Hecht | 90v-91 |
| O praise the Lord (Ps.147) | Willm Turner | 91 |
| By the waters of Babylon | William Turner | 91-91v |
| Out of the deep | Adrian Batten | 91v |
| I will give thanks (Ps.138) | John Cutts | 92 |

| | | |
|---|---|---|
| Lord, who shall dwell in thy tabernacle? | Andreas Hecht | 92-92v |
| The Lord is my light | Willm Laws | 92v |
| Lord, who shall dwell in thy tabernacle? | Mr Portmans | 92v-93 |
| Blessed is the man (Ps.1) | Mr Wise | 93 |
| Lord, what is man? | Wilm Turner | 93-93v |
| Lord, let me know mine end | (Matthew Lockes) | 93v-94 |
| O give thanks (Ps.107) | Willm Tucker | 94 |
| Wherewithal shall a young man cleanse his ways? | Willm Tucker | 94-94v |
| Lord, how are they increased | John Blow | 94v |
| Behold, how good and joyful a thing | John Blow | 94v |
| Awake up my glory | Michael Wise | 94v-95 |
| I will cry unto thee, O God | John Blow | 95 |
| God standeth in the congregation | Henry Hall | 95 |
| How are the mighty fallen | Michael Wise | 95v |
| Turn thee unto me | John Blow | 95v |
| Rejoice in the Lord, O ye righteous | Pelham Humfry | 95v |
| I will magnify thee | Will Tucker | 96 |
| I was glad | William Tucker | 96-96v |
| By the waters of Babylon | Michael Wise | 96v-97 |
| Christ being raised from the dead | John Blow | 97 |
| Blessed is he that considereth the poor | Michael Wise | 97-97v |
| O Lord, thou hast searched me out | Mr Blow | 97v |
| Rejoice in the Lord, O ye righteous | Richard Portman | 97v |
| Not unto us | Mr Lock | 98 |
| My God, my God, look upon me | Thos Tudway ('Organist of King's College in Cambridge') | 98-98v |
| This is the day | Will Tucker | 98v |
| Lord, how long wilt thou be angry? | Willm Tucker | 99 |
| O be joyful in the Lord | Pelham Humfrys | 99 |

| | | |
|---|---|---|
| Haste thee, O God | Pelham Humfrys | 99-99v |
| The earth is the Lord's | Dr Child | 99v |
| Turn thee unto me | John Blow | 99v-100 |
| O Lord our governor | Henry Pursell | 100 |
| I am well pleased | William Tucker | 100v |
| My heart is fixed | Willm Tucker | 100v |
| Sing we merrily | John Blow | 100v-101 |
| I will alway give thanks | Pelham Humfrys, Joh Blow, Willm Turner | 101 |
| Comfort ye, my people | Will Tucker | 101 |
| O praise the Lord, all ye heathen | Dr Christopher Gibbons | 101v |
| The Lord said unto my Lord | (Dr Christopher Gibbons) | 101v |
| Praise the Lord, ye servants | Will Tucker | 101v |
| Have mercy upon me | Pelham Humfrys | 101v-102 |
| O Lord, I have sinned | John Blow | 102-102v |
| Christ being raised from the dead | John Blow | 102v |
| By the waters of Babylon | Henry Hall | 102v |
| By the waters of Babylon | Mr Pelham Humfrys | 103 |
| Not unto us | (Matthew Lock) | 103-103v |
| Let God arise | Mr Willm Laws | 103v |
| Blow up the trumpet | Henry Pursel | 103v-104 |
| Let God arise | Henry Pursel | 104-104v |
| O how amiable are thy dwellings | Mr John Blow | 104v |
| Like as the hart | Pelham Humfrey | 105 |
| God be merciful unto us | Dr Christopher Gibbons | 105 |
| Blessed be the Lord my strength | Henry Purcell | 105-105v |
| Hear, O heavens | Pelham Humfrey | 105v |
| Lord, thou hast been our refuge | William Turner | 105v-106 |
| Lord, teach us to number | Mr Pelham Humfrys | 106 |
| O give thanks (Ps.118) ('This in Westminster books is on Cantoris Side & ye Verses are on yt side'.) | Pelham Humfrey | 106-106v |
| O Lord my God | Pelham Humfrys | 106v |

| | | |
|---|---|---|
| Let God arise | Dr Child | 107 |
| Sing unto the Lord, O ye saints | Dr Christopher Gibbons | 107 |
| Out of the deep | Willm Grigory | 107-107v |
| God be merciful unto us | John Blow | 107v |
| Thou art my King, O God | Dr Child | 107v |
| O God, thou hast cast us out | Willm Gregory | 107v |
| Behold, how good and joyful a thing | Dr Child | 107v-108 |
| Awake, awake, put on thy strength | Michael Wise | 108 |
| O praise the Lord, all ye heathen | Henry Pursel | 108 |
| *Prepare ye the way | Mr Wise | 108v |
| *O sing unto the Lord (Ps.98) | Dr Child | 108v |
| *O praise God in his holiness | Mr Wise | 108v |

Inside back cover: Eight Psalm Tunes (as for Medius Decani)

(3) Tenor Decani

Inside front cover: 'W.Gostling' and bookplate
ff. 1 - 4 blank


| | | |
|---|---|---|
| A Table of all ye Services & Anthems contained in this Book | | 5-6 |
| A Book of Services and Anthems for a Quire | | 6v |
| Mr Tallis's short Service (1,2,4,6,7,8,10) | | 7-8v |
| Mr Strogers short Service (1,2,4,6,7,8,10) | | 8v-10v |
| Mr Birds short Service (1,2,4,6,7,8,10) | | 10v-12 |
| Mr Thomas Tomkins's short Service (1,2,4,6,7,8,10) | | 12v-14 |
| Mr Bevin short Service (1,2,4,6,7,8,10) | | 14-15v |
| Mr Orlando Gibbons's short Service (1,2,4,6,7,8,10) | | 15v-17 |
| Mr Brynes short Service (2,5,6,7,8,10) | | 17-18 |
| Mr Ben Rogers short sharp Service (2,5,6,7,8,10) | | 18v-19v |
| Behold now, praise the Lord | Benjamin Rogers | 19v |
| Dr Childes sharp Service in D sol re (2,5,6,7,8,10) | | 19v-21 |
| Dr Childes Service in E minor (2,5,6,7,8,10) | | 21-22 |
| & allso Child's Service in F (2,5,6,7,9,11) | | 22-23v |
| Mr Richard Farrants high Service (2,4,6,7,8,10) | | 23v-25 |
| Mr Portmans Service (2,4,6,7,8,10) | | 25-26v |
| Mr Thomas Tomkins's Service in D minor (2,5,6,7,8,10) | | 26v-28v |
| Mr Reads Evening Service (8,10) | | 28v-29 |
| Mr Mundy's Service of 5. parts (1,2,4,6,7,8,10) | | 29-31v |
| Dr Rogers's Service in Gamut (2,4,6,7,8,10) | | 32-33 |
| Mr Pellham Humfreys short Service in E la mi (2,5,6,7,8,10) | | 33v-34v |
| Mr John Farrants short Service (2,5,6,7,8,10) | | 34v-35 |
| Mr Adrian Battens short Service (2,5,6,7,8,10) | | 35-36 |
| Dr Rogers's Service in E la mi (2,5,6,7,8,10) | | 36-37 |
| Mr Blows short Service in G (2,5,8,10) | | 37-37v |
| Mr Patricks short Service (2,4,6,8,10) | | 38-38v |
| Dr Childs Benedicite Service (3,5,6,7,8,10) | | 38v-39v |
| Mr Tuckers Benedicite Service (3,5,6,7,8,10) | | 39v-40v |
| John Amners Caesar's Service (2,5,6,7,8,10) | | 40v-42v |
| O come hither, and hearken | John Amner | 42v |
| Mr John Amner's Service of 4 parts (2,4,6,7,8,10) | | 42v-44 |

| | | |
|---|---|---|
| Mr Patricks Kiery & Creed (for Cantoris side) (6,7) | | 44-44v |
| Mr Blows Service in A re (2,5,6,7,9,11) | | 44v-45v |
| Mr Wises Morning & Evening Service in D minor (2,5,6,8,10) | | 45v-46 |
| Dr Childs Service in A re (i.e., A minor) (2,5,6,7,8,10) | | 46-46v |
| Dr Childs Te Deum to his Benedicite Service in Gamut (2) | | 47 |
| Dr Childs verse Evening Service (9) | | 47 |
| The Commandments & Creed of Mr Blows Service in G | | 47v |
| This following belongs to ye next foregoing Service of Dr Childs (11) | | 47v |
| Mr John Blow's Service in E minor or his Benedicite Service (3,5,6,7,9,11) | | 48-49v |
| & his (John Blow's) Second Commandments & Creed in G | | 49v |
| 'Full Anthems of 4 parts' (heading) | | 50 |
| Almighty God, we beseech thee, give ear | Thos Heardson | 50 |
| O Lord, give thy holy spirit | Thos Tallis | 50 |
| O God, be merciful unto us | Nicholas Strogers | 50 |
| Call to remembrance | Richard Farrant | 50v |
| Keep, we beseech thee, O good Lord | Thos Heardson | 50v |
| Hide not thou thy face | Richard Farrant | 50v |
| I will exalt thee (with 2nd part,'Sing unto the Lord') | Dr Tye | 50v-51 |
| O Lord, the maker of all thing | Wm Mundy | 51 |
| O Lord, the world's Saviour | Willm Mundy | 51v |
| Teach me thy way | Edmund Hooper | 51v |
| Almighty and everlasting God | Orlando Gibbons | 51v-52 |
| O praise the Lord, all ye heathen | Adrian Batten | 52 |
| Deliver us, O Lord our God (with 2nd part,'Blessed be the Lord God of Israel') | Orlando Gibbons | 52 |
| Hide not thou thy face | Adrian Batten | 52-52v |
| Lord, we beseech thee give ear | Adrian Batten | 52v |
| Haste thee, O God (with 2nd part,'But let all those that seek') | Adrian Batten | 52v |

| | | |
|---|---|---|
| When the Lord turned again the captivity | Adrian Batten | 52v |
| O God, whose never failing providence | Andreas Hecht | 53 |
| Blow out the trumpet | Martin Peerson | 53 |
| I give you a new commandment | John Cutts | 53 |
| Behold, how good and joyful a thing | Willm Turner | 53v |
| Sing, O daughter of Zion | Willm Turner | 53v |
| O give thanks (Ps.107) | Dr Rogers's | 53v-54 |
| Let thy merciful ears | John Cutts | 54 |
| My soul truly waiteth | Mr Batten | 54 |
| Deliver us, O Lord | Adrian Batten | 54 |
| O sing joyfully | Adrian Batten | 54v |
| O clap your hands | Dr Wm Child | 54v |
| O pray for the peace of Jerusalem | Dr Wm Child | 54v |
| O Lord, grant the king a long life | William Child | 55 |
| If the Lord himself | William Child | 55 |
| O give thanks (Ps.105) | Willm Tucker | 55v |
| Praise the Lord, O my soul (Ps.103) | Dr Child | 55v |
| Teach me, O Lord | Dr Rogers | 56 |
| O God, the King of glory | Henry Pursel | 56 |
| The Lord hear thee | Mr John Blow | 56-56v |
| Let my complaint come before thee | Adrian Batten | 56v |
| O Lord God of hosts | Willm Turner | 56v |
| 'Full Anthems of 5 parts' (heading) | | 57 |
| With all our hearts | Thos Tallis | 57 |
| Blessed be thy name, O God | Thos Tallis | 57 |
| O thou God, Almighty Father | Edmund Hooper | 57 |
| O Lord, I bow the knees of my heart | Wm Mundy | 57-57v |
| I call and cry | Thos Tallis | 57v |
| Pevent us, O Lord | Willm Bird | 57v-58 |
| Behold, it is Christ | Edmund Hooper | 58 |
| O Lord, make thy servant Charles | Willm Bird | 58 |

| | | |
|---|---|---|
| I lift my heart to thee | Dr Tye | 58v |
| O Lord, turn thy wrath (with 2nd part,'Bow thine ear') | Willm Bird | 58v-59 |
| O give thanks | Dr Giles | 59 |
| O come, let us sing unto the Lord | Robert Ramsey | 59v |
| Why art thou so full of heaviness? | Thos Wilkinson | 59v |
| O Jerusalem, thou that killest the prophets | Thos Wilkinson | 59v-60 |
| Almighty God, the fountain of all wisdom | Thos Tomkins | 60 |
| Hear my prayer, O God | Adrian Batten | 60-60v |
| We beseech thee, Almighty God | Adrian Batten | 60v |
| The Lord bless us | Willm White | 60v-61 |
| O clap your hands | Willm Tucker | 61 |
| I will sing unto the Lord | Henry Pursell | 61-61v |
| Save me, O God (Ps.69) | John Blow | 61v |
| Save me, O God (Ps.54) | Henry Pursel | 61v |
| *Mr Purcells Service in B flat (2,4,6,7,8,10) | | 62 |
| 'Anthems of 6 & 7 parts' (heading) | | 63 |
| Deliver me from mine enemies | Robert Parsons | 63 |
| Sing joyfully | Willm Bird | 63 |
| Lord, who shall dwell in thy tabernacle? | Adrian Batten | 63-63v |
| O clap your hands | Adrian Batten | 63v |
| Hosanna to the Son of David | Orlando Gibbons | 63v-64 |
| Lift up your heads | Orlando Gibbons | 64 |
| The King shall rejoice | John Tomkins | 64-64v |
| O clap your hands (Dr Heathers commencement Song composed by Orlando Gibbons) | | 64v |
| Inclina Domine (Mr Robert Ramsys Commencement Song of 8 pts) | | 65 |
| O praise God in his holiness | Willm White | 65v |
| *Blessed is the man (Ps.1) | John Sargenson | 65v-66 |
| *Try me, O God | Dr Turner | 66 |

ff. 66v, 67 blank

| | | |
|---|---|---|
| Lord, I am not high minded | Dr Christopher Gibbons's | 68 |
| *Praise the Lord, O my soul (Ps.146) | Henry Loosemore | 68 |
| Unto thee, O Lord, will I lift up | Richard Deering | 68v |
| God is our hope and strength | John Blow | 68v |
| Holy, holy, holy | Mr Baten | 68v |
| O God, whose never failing providence | Andreas Hecht | 69 |
| In thee, O Lord, do I put my trust | Dr Bull | 69 |
| Save me, O God (Ps.54) | Willm Bird | 69 |
| Unto thee, O Lord, do I lift up | Willm Tucker | 69v |
| O be joyful in God | Willm Turner | 69v |
| Behold, I bring you good tidings | Ben Rogers | 70 |
| Sing unto the Lord, O ye kingdoms | Willm Turner | 70 |
| This is the day | W. Turner | 70-70v |
| Praise the Lord, O my soul (Ps.103) | Andreas Hecht | 70v |
| Above the stars the Saviour dwells | Dr Christopher Gibbons | 70v-71 |
| My days are gone | John Cutts | 71 |
| O praise the Lord, ye angels | John Cutts | 71 |
| O sing unto the Lord (Ps.98) | John Cutts | 71 |
| O praise the Lord (Ps.147) | Wilm Turner | 71v |
| Hear my crying, O God | Andreas Hecht | 71v |
| By the waters of Babylon | John Cutts | 71v |
| Praise the Lord, ye servants | Andreas Hecht | 71v-72 |
| Comfort ye, my people | Wilm Tucker | 72 |
| Lord, who shall dwell in thy tabernacle? | Andreas Hecht | 72 |
| Haste thee, O God | Andreas Hecht | 72 |
| Look, shepherds, look | Unattributed | 72v-73 |
| Behold, I bring you glad tidings | Orlando Gibbons | 73 |

| | | |
|---|---|---|
| I heard a voice in heaven saying, Allelujah | Albertus Bryne | 73-73v |
| O that mine eyes would melt | George Loosmore | 73v |
| Blessed is the man (Ps.1) | Andreas Hecht | 74 |
| Almighty God, which by the leading of a star | Dr Bull | 74v |
| Out of the deep | Thomas Morley | 74v |
| Behold, thou hast made my days | Orlando Gibbons | 75 |
| Blessed are all they | Orlando Gibbons | 75v |
| O Lord, let me know mine end | Thos Tomkins | 75v-76 |
| O Lord, make thy servant Charles | Willm Cranford | 76-76v |
| Bow down thine ear | John Ward | 76v-77 |
| I will magnify thee | John Cutts | 77 |
| My song shall be of mercy | Henry Lawes | 77v |
| Now that the Lord hath readvanced the crown | William King | 78 |
| Out of the deep | Adrian Batten | 78-78v |
| Glorious and powerful God | Orlando Gibbons | 78v |
| Thou art my King, O God | Thos tomkins | 79 |
| O Lord our governor | Adrian Batten | 79-79v |
| My beloved spake | Thos tomkins | 79v-80 |
| I will praise the Lord | John Ward | 80-80v |
| O how amiable are thy dwellings | Mr Loe | 80v |
| How long wilt thou forget me? | Albert Bryne | 80v-81 |
| Let God arise | John Ward | 81-81v |
| O praise God in his holiness | Edward Smith | 81v |
| O how happy a thing it is | Adrian Batten | 82 |
| Let all the world in every corner sing | Henry Loosmore | 82 |
| Preserve me, O Lord | Thos Wilkinson | 82-82v |
| Hear my prayer, O Lord, and let thine ear | Thos Wilkinson | 82v |
| Save me, O God (Ps.54) | Willm Bird | 82v-83 |
| Zadok the priest | Henry Lawes | 83 |
| How long wilt thou forget me? | Dr Christopher Gibbons | 83 |
| If ye be risen again | Orlando Gibbons | 83 |
| How long wilt thou forget me? | Mr Morley | 83v |
| The earth is the Lord's | Willm Turner | 83v |

| | | |
|---|---|---|
| Christ rising again | Mr Batten | 84 |
| By the waters of Babylon | Willm Turner | 84-84v |
| I will give thanks (Ps.138) | John Cutts | 84v |
| O sing unto the Lord (Ps.149) | Willm King | 84v |
| The Lord is my light | Willm Lawes | 85 |
| O come hither, and hearken | John Cutts | 85 |
| Lord, how long wilt thou be angry? | Willm Tucker | 85v |
| Praise the Lord, ye servants | William Tucker | 85v |
| Lord, who shall dwell in thy tabernacle? | Mr Portmans | 86 |
| Blessed is the man (Ps.1) | (Michael Wise) | 86-86v |
| Lord, what is man? | Willm Turner | 86v |
| Lord, let me know mine end | (Mr Lock) | 86v-87 |
| Turn thy face from my sins | Matthew Locke | 87-87v |
| O give thanks (Ps. 107) | Willm Tucker | 87v |
| Lord, how are they increased | John Blow | 87v-88 |
| Wherewithal shall a young man mend his ways? | Will Tucker | 88 |
| Behold, how good and joyful a thing | John Blow | 88-88v |
| Awake up, my glory | Michael Wise | 88v |
| God standeth in the congregation | Henry Hall | 88v |
| I will cry unto thee, O God | (John Blow) | 88v-89 |
| How are the mighty fallen | Michael Wise | 89-89v |
| Turn thee unto me | John Blow | 89v |
| Rejoice in the Lord, O ye righteous | Pellham Humfreys | 89v-90 |
| I will magnify thee | Will Tucker | 90-90v |
| I was glad | Will Tucker | 90v |
| By the waters of Babylon | Michael Wise | 90v |
| Christ being raised from the dead | John Blow | 90v-91 |
| Blessed is he that considereth the poor | Michael Wise | 91 |
| The Lord said unto my Lord | (Dr Christopher Gibbons) | 91 |

| | | |
|---|---|---|
| O Lord, thou hast searched me out | John Blow | 91v |
| Rejoice in the Lord, O ye righteous | Richard Portman | 91v |
| Not unto us | Matthew Lock | 91v-92 |
| The earth is the Lord's | Dr Child | 92 |
| My God, my God, look upon me | Thos Tudway | 92v-93 |
| This is the day | Willm Tucker | 93 |
| Haste thee, O God | Pellham Humfreys | 93-93v |
| I am well pleased | Willm Tucker | 93v |
| O Lord our governor | Henry Pursel | 93v-94 |
| My heart is fixed | Willm Tucker | 94 |
| Sing we merrily | John Blow | 94-94v |
| I will alway give thanks | Pelham Humfrey, William Turner, John Blow | 94v |
| Haste thee, O God | Pelham Humfrey | 94v-95 |
| O praise the Lord, all ye heathen | Dr Christopher Gibbons | 95 |
| Have mercy upon me | Pelham Humfrys | 95-95v |
| O Lord, I have sinned | John Blow | 95v |
| Christ being raised from the dead | John Blow | 95v-96 |
| Behold, God is my salvation | Willm Turner | 96-96v |
| By the waters of Babylon | Pellham Humfrys | 96v |
| Not unto us | Matthew Lock | 97 |
| Let God arise | Willm Laws | 97 |
| Blow up the trumpet | Henry Pursell | 97-97v |
| Let God arise | Henry Pursel | 97v-98 |
| Blessed be the Lord, my strength | Henry Pursel | 98 |
| Hear, O heavens | Mr Humfrys | 98-98v |
| O how amiable are thy dwellings | Mr Blow | 98v |
| Lord, thou hast been our refuge | Willm Turner | 98v-99 |
| Behold, God is my salvation | Mr Tudway | 99 |
| Lord, teach us to number our days | Mr Pellham Humfrys | 99-99v |

| | | |
|---|---|---|
| O give thanks (Ps.118) | Pelham Humfrys | 99v |
| Like as the hart | Pellham Humfrys | 99v-100 |
| O God, wherefore art thou absent? | John Blow | 100 |
| God be merciful unto us | Dr Christopher Gibbons | 100-100v |
| O Lord, rebuke me not | Dr Childs | 100v |
| Behold, how good and joyful a thing | (Dr Child) | 100v |
| O Lord my God | Mr Pellham Humfry | 100v |
| Let God arise | Dr Child | 100v |
| Out of the deep | Willm Grigory | 101 |
| God be merciful unto us | John Blow | 101 |
| Thou art my King, O God | Dr Child | 101 |
| O God, thou hast cast us out | Willm Grigory | 101-101v |
| Awake, awake, put on thy strength | Michael Wise | 101v-102 |
| O praise the Lord, all ye heathen | Henry Pursel | 102-102v |
| The Commandments & Creed of Mr Wises in D sol re to his Service page 78 (f.45v). It should be on Cantoris side. | | 102v |
| His (Michael Wise's) Commandments & Creed in E la mi sharp (i.e., in E major) | | 102v-103 |
| Dr Blows Te Deum to his Service in E minor | | 103-103v |
| Mr Aldridgs Benedicite Service (3,5,6,7,8,10) | | 103v-104 |
| Mr Ferabosco's Evening Service (8,10) | | 104-104v |
| Mr Aldridg's Service in Gamut (2,5,6,7,8,10) | | 104v-105 |
| *Verse belonging to O give thanks (Ps.118) | Pelham Humfrey | 105 |
| ff.105v, 106 blank | | |
| Mr Tallis's Te Deum and Benedictus for both sides | | 107-107v |
| Dr Childs flatt Service in E (2,5,6,7,8,10) | | 107v-108 |
| The Epiphany Anthem for me Tenor Decani as its in ye Westminster books (Almighty God, who by the leading of a star) | John Bull | 108v |
| ff.109-112 blank | | |
| Inside back cover: Eight Psalm Tunes (as for Medius Decani) | | |

(4) Bass Decani

Inside front cover: Signature 'W.Gostling' and bookplate
Fly-leaf

| | |
|---|---|
| A Table of all ye Services contained in ys Book | 1 |
| A Table of all ye Anthems contained in ys Book | 1v-3v |
| Mr Tallis his short service (1,2,4,6,7,8,10) | 4-5v |
| Mr Strogers his short service (1,2,4,6,7,8,10) | 5v-7v |
| Mr Birds short service (1,2,4,6,7,8,10) | 7v-9v |
| Mr Thomas Tomkins Short Service (1,2,4,6,7,8,10) | 9v-11 |
| Mr Bevins Short Service (1,2,4,6,7,8,10) | 11-13 |
| Mr Orlando Gibbons his short Service(1,2,4,6,7,8,10) | 13v-14 |
| Mr Brynes Short Service (2,5,6,7,8,10) | 14v-15v |
| Mr Ben Rogers short sharp Service (2,5,6,7,8,10) | 16-17 |
| Behold now, praise the Lord Benjamin Rogers (note at end: 'The end of Mr Rogers short sharp Service') | 17 |
| Dr Child's sharp Service in D sol re (2,5,6,7,8,10) | 17-18v |
| as also Dr Child's in E minor (2,5,6,7,8,10) | 18v-19v |
| Dr Child's Service in F (2,5,6,7,9,11) | 19v-21 |
| Mr Richard Farrants high Service (2,4,6,7,8,10) | 21-23v |
| Mr Portman's Service (2,4,6,7,8,10) | 23-24 |
| Mr Thomas Tomkins's Service in D minor (2,5,6,7,8,10) | 24-25 |
| Mr Mundy's Service for 5 Parts 2 Contratenors (1,2,4,6,7,8,10) | 25v-27v |
| Dr Rogers's Service in Gamut (2,5,6,7,8,10) | 27v-28v |
| Mr Pellam Humfreys short Service in E minor (2,5,6,7,8,10) | 29-29v |
| Mr John Farrants Short Service (2,5,6,7,8,10) | 29v-30 |
| Adrian Batten's short Service (2,5,6,7,8,10) | 30-30v |
| Dr Roger's Service in E la mi (2,5,6,7,8,10) | 31-31v |
| Mr Blow's Service in G (2,5,8,10) | 31v-32 |
| Mr Patricks Service (2,4,6,8,10) | 32-32v |
| Dr Child's Benedicite Service (3,5,6,7,8,10) | 33-33v |
| Mr Tuckers Benedicite Service (3,5,8,10) | 33v-34v |
| Mr Tuckers Short Service (2,5,8,10) | 34v-35 |
| John Amners Caesars Service (2,5,6,7,8,10) | 35-36v |
| Mr John Amners Service of 4 Parts (2,4,6,7,8,10) | 36v-38 |
| O come hither, and hearken John Amner | 36v |

| | | |
|---|---|---|
| Mr Patricks Kyrie & Creed | | 38-38v |
| Mr John Blows Service in A re (2,5,6,7,9,11) | | 38v-39v |
| Mr Wises Morning & Evening Service in D sol re (2,5,8,10) | | 39v-40 |
| Dr Childs Service in A re (i.e., A minor) (2,5,6,7,8,10) | | 40-40v |
| Dr Childs Flatt Service in E (2,5,6,7,8,10) | | 40v-41 |
| Dr Childs Te Deum to his Benedicite Service in Gamut & his Evening Service for verses in G (2,9,11) | | 41v-42 |
| Mr John Blows Service in E minor or his Benedicite Service (3,5,6,7,9,11) | | 42-43v |
| The Creed to his (John Blow's) Service in G (6,7) | | 43v-44 |
| Mr Wises Sharp Creed in E la mi (i.e.,E major) (6,7) & his in D sol re (6,7) | | 44-44v |
| Dr Blow's Te Deum to his Benedicite Service | | 44v-45 |
| Mr Henry Aldridg's Benedicite Service in E la mi (3,5,6,7,8,10) | | 45-45v |
| Mr Joh Ferabosco's Evening Service for verses (8,10) | | 45v |
| Mr Aldridg's Service in Gamut (2,5,6,7,8,10) | | 45v-46 |
| Dr Blow's Second Creed in Gamut (triple time) (6,7) | | 46v |
| *Mr Purcells service in B flat (2,4,6,7,8,10) | | 46v-48 |
| *Dr Blow's Te Deum to his Service in E la mi | | 48 |
| ff.48v, 49 blank | | |
| 'Full Anthems of 4 Parts' (heading) | | 50 |
| Almighty God, we beseech thee, give ear | Thos Heardson | 50 |
| O Lord, give thy holy spirit | Thos Tallis | 50 |
| O God, be merciful unto us | Nicholas Strogers | 50 |
| Call to remembrance | Richard Farrant | 50v |
| Keep, we beseech thee, O good Lord | Thomas Heardson | 50v |
| Hide not thou thy face | (Mr Richard Farrant) | 50v |
| I will exalt thee (with 2nd part,'Sing unto the Lord') | Dr Tye | 50v-51 |
| O Lord, the maker of all thing | Willm Mundy | 51 |
| O Lord, the world's saviour | Willm Mundy | 51v |
| Teach me thy way | Richard Farrant (recte E.Hooper) | 51v |
| Almighty and everlasting God | Orlando Gibbons | 51v |

| | | |
|---|---|---|
| O praise the Lord, all ye heathen | Adrian Batten | 52 |
| Deliver us, O Lord (with 2nd part,'Blessed be the Lord God') | Orlando Gibbons | 52 |
| Hide not thou thy face (with 2nd part,'Lord, we beseech thee') | Adrian Batten | 52-52v |
| Haste thee, O God (with 2nd part,'But let all those that seek thee') | Adrian Batten | 52v |
| When the Lord turned again the captivity | Adrian Batten | 52v |
| Blow out the trumpet | Martin Pearson | 52v-53 |
| O God, whose never failing providence | Andreas Hecht | 53 |
| Zadok the priest | Henry Lawes | 53 |
| I give you a new commandment | John Cutts | 53 |
| Sing, O daughter of Zion | Willm Turner | 53v |
| Deliver us, O Lord | Adrian Batten | 53v |
| My soul truly waiteth | Adrian Batten | 53v |
| O sing joyfully | Adrian Batten | 53v-54 |
| Praise the Lord, O my soul (Ps.103) | Dr Child | 54 |
| O Lord, grant the king a long life | Dr Child | 54 |
| If the Lord himself | Dr Child | 54v |
| O clap your hands | Dr Child | 54v |
| Let my complaint come before thee | Adrian Batten | 54v-55 |
| O give thanks (Ps.105) (ending only; see f.68 below) | Willm Tucker | 55 |
| O pray for the peace of Jerusalem | Dr Child | 55 |
| Teach me, O Lord | Dr Rogers | 55 |
| O God, the king of glory | Henry Pursell | 55v |
| The Lord hear thee | Mr John Blow | 55v |
| *I was glad | Mr Purcell | 55v-56 |
| *O give thanks (Ps.106) | (Mr Purcell) | 56v-57 |
| *Behold, I bring you glad tidings | Mr Purcell | 57v-58 |
| *Try me, O God | Dr Turner | 58 |

| | | |
|---|---|---|
| *Out of the deep | Dr Aldrich | 58v |
| *O praise the Lord (Ps.135) | Dr Child | 58v-59 |
| *O God, to whom vengeance belongeth | J sine nomine B (recte John Blow?) | 59 |
| ff.59v,60, 61, 62,63 blank | | |
| 'Full Anthems of 5 Parts' (heading) | | 64 |
| With all our hearts | Thos Tallis | 64 |
| Blessed be thy name, O God | Thos Tallis | 64 |
| O thou God, Almighty Father | Edmund Hooper | 64 |
| I call and cry | Thos Tallis | 64-64v |
| O Lord, I bow the knees of my heart | Willm Mundy | 64v |
| Prevent us, O Lord | Willm Bird | 64v-65 |
| Behold, it is Christ | Edmund Hooper | 65 |
| O Lord, make thy servant Charles | (William Bird) | 65 |
| I lift my heart to thee ɜe | Dr Tye | 65-65v |
| O Lord, turn thy wrath (with 2nd part,'Bow thine ear') | Willm Bird | 65v |
| O give thanks | Dr Giles | 65v-66 |
| O come, let us sing unto the Lord | Robert Ramsey | 66 |
| O Jerusalem, thou that killest the prophets | Mr Wilkinson | 66-66v |
| Why art thou so full of heaviness? | Mr Wilkinson | 66v |
| Almighty God, the fountain of all wisdom | Thos Tomkins | 66v |
| Save me, O God (Ps.54) | Willm Bird | 67 |
| Hear my prayer, O God | Adrian Batten | 67 |
| We beseech thee, Almighty God | Mr Batten | 67-67v |
| Hear my prayer, O God | Adrian Batten | 67v |
| O give thanks (Ps.105) | Will Tucker | 67v-68 |
| The Lord bless us | Willm White | 68 |
| O clap your hands | Willm Tucker | 68 |
| I will sing unto the Lord | Henry Pursell | 68v |
| O Lord, I have loved the habitation | Thos Tomkins | 68v |

| | | |
|---|---|---|
| Save me, O God (Ps.54) | Henry Pursell | 68v-69 |
| *O praise God in his holiness | Mr Wise | 69-69v |
| *O clap your hands | Dr Rogers | 69v |
| *The Lord said unto my Lord | (Mr Wise) | 69v-70 |
| *Thy way, O God, is holy | Henry Purcell | 70-70v |
| *I waited patiently | Dr Blow | 71 |
| *When the Son of Man shall come | Dr Blow | 71-71v |
| *O be joyful in God | Dr Blow | 71v-72 |
| *Thy word is a lantern (incomplete) | Henry Purcell | 72v |
| f.73 recto blank | | |
| O praise God in his holiness | Mr White | 73v |
| f.74 recto blank | | |
| Mr Robert Ramsys Commencement Song of 8 Parts Inclina Domine | | 74v |
| Dr Heathers Commencement Song composed by Mr Orlando Gibbons, O clap your hands | | 75 |
| The king shall rejoice | John Tompkins | 75v |
| God is our hope and strength (a 8) | Mr John Blow | 75v |
| 'Full Anthems of 6 Parts' (heading) | | |
| Sing joyfully | Willm Bird | 76 |
| Deliver me from mine enemies | Robert Parsons | 76 |
| Hosanna to the Son of David | Orlando Gibbons | 76-76v |
| Lift up your heads | Orlando Gibbons | 76v |
| O Lord, grant the king a long life | Thomas Weelks | 76v |
| O clap your hands | Adrian Batten | 76v-77 |
| Lord, who shall dwell in thy tabernacle? | Adrian Batten | 77 |
| O Lord, thou hast searched me out | Adrian Batten | 77-77v |
| Lord, let me know mine end | (Matthew Lock) | 77v-78 |
| My beloved spake | Thomas Tomkins | 78 |
| *Teach me, O Lord | Dr Christopher Gibbons | 78 |
| ff.78v, 79 blank | | |
| Blessed is he that considereth the poor | Michael Wise | 80 |

| | | |
|---|---|---|
| Out of the deep | Thos Morley | 80v |
| Out of the deep | Adrian Batten | 80v |
| I will praise the Lord | John Ward | 80v-81 |
| Holy, holy, holy | Adrian Batten | 81 |
| Unto thee, O Lord, will I lift up | Richard Deering | 81 |
| If ye be risen again with Christ | Orlando Gibbons | 81v |
| Behold, I bring you glad tidings | Orlando Gibbons | 81v |
| Glorious and powerful God | Orlando Gibbons | 81v-82 |
| Behold, God is my salvation | Willm Turner | 82-82v |
| Haste thee, O God | Andrew Hecht | 82v |
| Praise the Lord, ye servants | Andrew Hecht | 83 |
| Unto thee, O Lord, do I lift up | Mr Willm Tucker | 83v |
| Hear my crying, O God (completed at foot of f.83) | Andrew Hecht | 83v |
| 'Verse Anthems' (heading) | | 84 |
| Almighty God, who by the leading of a star | Dr Bull | 84 |
| In thee, O Lord, put I my trust | Dr Bull | 84 |
| Behold, thou hast made my days | Orlando Gibbons | 84-84v |
| Blessed are all they ('Here is a semibreve rest more yn is in ye Chapel Books') | Orlando Gibbons | 84v |
| The Lord is my light | William Lawes | 84v-85 |
| O come hither and hearken | (John Cutts) | 85-85v |
| Lord, how long wilt thou be angry | Willm Tucker | 85v |
| Praise the Lord, ye servants | Willm Tucker | 85v |
| How long wilt thou forget me? | Albertus Bryne | 85v-86 |
| Lord, who shall dwell in thy tabernacle? | Mr Portmans | 86 |
| I heard a voice from heaven saying, Allelujah | Albertus Bryne | 86-86v |

| | | |
|---|---|---|
| Blessed is the man (Ps.1) | Mr Wise | 86v-87 |
| Lord, what is man? | Willm Turner | 87-87v |
| Turn thy face from my sins | Matthew Lock | 87v |
| O give thanks (Ps.107) | Wilm Tucker | 87v |
| Wherewithal shall a young man cleanse? | Willm Tucker | 88 |
| Behold, how good and joyful a thing | John Blow | 88 |
| Awake up my glory | Michael Wise | 88 |
| God standeth in the congregation | Henry Hall | 88v |
| I will cry unto thee, O God | John Blow | 88v |
| How are the mighty fallen | Michael Wise | 88v |
| Turn thee unto me | Joh Blow | 88v-89 |
| Rejoice in the Lord, O ye righteous | Pelham Humfrey | 89 |
| I will magnify thee | Will Tucker | 89-89v |
| I was glad | Will Tucker | 89v |
| By the waters of Babylon | Michael Wise | 90 |
| Christ being raised from the dead | John Blow | 90-90v |
| The Lord said unto my Lord | Dr Christopher Gibbons | 90v |
| O Lord, thou hast searched me out | John Blow | 90v-91 |
| Rejoice in the Lord, O ye righteous | Richard Portman | 91v |
| Not unto us | Matthew Lock | 91v |
| The earth is the Lord's | Dr Child | 92 |
| O be joyful in the Lord | Pelham Humfreys | 92-92v |
| Let God arise | John Ward | 92v-93 |
| O Lord, make thy servant Charles | Mr Cranford | 93-93v |
| My song shall be of mercy | Henry Laws | 93v |
| Above the stars the Saviour dwells | Dr Christopher Gibbons | 93v-94 |
| How long wilt thou forget me? | Dr Christopher Gibbons | 94 |
| My God, my God, look upon me | Thomas Tudway ('Organist of King's College in Cambridge') | 94-94v |

| | | |
|---|---|---|
| This is the day | Willm Tucker | 94v-95 |
| Lord, how are they increased | John Blow | 95 |
| Haste thee, O God | Pellham Humfry's | 95-95v |
| Comfort ye, my people | Willm Tucker | 95v |
| O Lord our governor | Henry Pursell | 96-96v |
| My heart is fixed | Willm Tucker | 96v |
| Sing we merrily | John Blow | 97 |
| I will alway give thanks | Pellam Humfrys, John Blow, Willm Turner | 97-97v |
| I am well pleased | Willm Tucker | 97v-98 |
| O praise the Lord, all ye heathen | Dr Christopher Gibbons | 98 |
| Have mercy upon me | Pellham Humfrys | 98-98v |
| O Lord, I have sinned | Mr John Blow | 98v-99 |
| Christ being raised from the dead | John Blow | 99 |
| O Lord our governor (incomplete) | (Adrian Batten) | 99v |
| By the waters of Babylon | Mr Pellham Humfrys | 99v-100 |
| Not unto us | Matthew Lock | 100-100v |
| Let God arise | Willm Laws | 100v-101 |
| Blow up the trumpet | Henry Purcell | 101 |
| Let God arise | Henry Pursell | 101v |
| Blessed be the Lord my strength | Henry Pursel | 101v-102 |
| Hear, O heavens | Pellham Humfry | 102 |
| O how amiable are thy dwellings | John Blow | 102-102v |
| Lord, thou hast been our refuge | Willm Turner | 102v-103 |
| Behold, God is my salvation | Thos Tudway | 103 |
| Lord, teach us to number our days | Pelham Humfrys | 103-103v |
| O give thanks (Ps.118) | Mr Pelham Humfrys | 103v-104 |
| Like as the hart | Mr Humfry's | 104-104v |
| O God, wherefore art thou absent? | Mr Blow | 104v |
| O Lord God of hosts | Willm Turner | 104v-105 |

| | | |
|---|---|---|
| Save me, O God (Ps.69) | Mr John Blow | 105 |
| God be merciful unto us | Dr Christopher Gibbons | 105-105v |
| O Lord, rebuke me not | Dr Childs | 105v |
| Behold, how good and joyful a thing | Dr Childs | 106 |
| O Lord my God | Mr Pellham Humfry's | 106-106v |
| Lord, I am not high minded | Dr Christopher Gibbons's | 106v |
| Let God arise | Dr Childs | 106v-107 |
| Sing unto the Lord, O ye saints | Dr Christopher Gibbons | 107 |
| Out of the deep | Willm Grigory | 107-107v |
| God be merciful unto us | John Blow | 107v |
| Thou art my king, O God | Dr Child | 107v |
| O God, thou hast cast us out | W.Grigoris | 108 |
| Awake, awake, put on thy strength | Michael Wise | 108v |
| O praise the Lord, all ye heathen (incomplete) | Henry Pursel | 108v |
| *Prepare ye the way | Mr Wise | 109 |
| *O sing unto the Lord (Ps.98) | Dr Child | 109 |

f.109 blank

Inside back cover: Eight Psalm Tunes (as for Medius Decani)

(5) Medius Cantoris

Inside front cover: Signature 'W.Gostling' and bookplate
Fly-leaf
A Table of all ye Services contained in ys Book 2

f. 2v blank

A Table of all ye Anthems contained in ys Book 3-5

f. 5v blank

Mr Thos Tallis short Service (1,2,4,6,7,8,10) 6-7v

Mr Nicholas Strogers short Service (1,2,4,6,7,8,10) 7v-10

Mr Willm Birds short Service (1,2,4,6,7,8,10) 10-12

Mr Bevins short Service (1,2,4,6,7,8,10) 12-14

Mr Thos Tomkins's short Service (1,2,4,6,7,8,10) 14-16

Mr Orlando Gibbons short Service (1,2,4,6,7,8,10) 16-18

Mr Albertus Brynes short Service (2,5,6,7,8,10) 18-19v

Benjamin Rogers sharp Service (2,5,6,7,8,10) 19v-21

Behold now, praise the Lord (Dr Rogers) 21-21v
(at the close of this item:'The end of Mr Rogers short sharp service')

Dr Childes sharp Service in D sol re (2,5,6,7,8,10) 21v-23

Dr Childes Service in E minor (2,5,6,7,8,10) 23-25

Dr Child's Service in F (2,5,6,7,9,11) 25-26v

Mr Richard Farrants high Service (2,4,6,7,8,10) 26v-29
(note: 'This Creed is to be on Decani side accordg to Mr Tuckers books')

Mr Portmans Service (2,4,6,7,8,10) 29v-31

Mr Thomas Thomkins Service in D minor (2,5,6,7,8,10) 31-32

Dr Rogers Service in Gamut (2,5,6,7,8,10) 32v-34

Mr Pellam Humfreys short Service in E minor 34-35
(2,5,6,7,8,10)
(note at head: 'This part for ye Service is on Decani side in Westminster Books'; to 8: 'This verse is put on Cantoris side in Westminster Books')

Mr John Farrants short Service (2,5,6,7,8,10) 35v-36

Mr Battens short Service (2,5,6,7,8,10) 36-37

Dr Rogers's Service in E la mi (2,5,6,7,8,10) 37-38

Mr Blow's short Service in G (2,5,8,10) 38-38v

Dr Rogers's Service in E la mi (2,5,8,10) 38v-39

Mr Patricks Service (2,4,8,10) 39v-40

Dr Childs Benedicite Service (3,5,6,7,8,10) 40-41

| | | |
|---|---|---|
| Mr Tuckers Benedicite Service (3,5,6,7,8,10) | | 41-42v |
| Mr Willm Tuckers short Service (2,5,8,10) | | 42v-43 |
| Mr John Amners Service called Caesar's (2,5,6,7,8,10) | | 43v-45 |
| O come hither and hearken ('The Anthem to the Service') | John Amner | 45 |
| Mr Patricks Commandments & Creed | | 45v |
| Mr John Blow's Service in A re (2,5,6,7,9,11) | | 45v-46v |
| Mr Michael Wises Morning & Evening Service in D minor (2,5,8,10) | | 47-47v |
| Dr Childs Te Deum to his Benedicite Service | | 47v |
| Dr Childs Service in A re (l.e., A minor) (2,5,6,7,8,10) | | 47v-48 |
| Dr Childs flatt Service in E la mi (2,5,6,7,8,10) | | 48v-49 |
| Dr Childs Evening Service in Gamut (9,11) | | 49-49v |
| Mr Blows Service in E minor or his Benedicite Service (3,5,6,7,9,11) | | 50-51 |
| Commandments & Creed to Mr Blows Service in G | | 51-51v |
| The Commandments & Creed to Mr Wises Service in D minor | | 51v |
| The Commandments & Creed of Mr Wises Service in E sharp (l.e., E major) | | 51v-52 |
| Dr Blows Te Deum to his E la mi Service This appears to have been inserted later than the preceding or immediately succeeding items. | | 52 |
| Mr John Ferabosco's Evening Service for Verses (8,10) | | 52v |
| Mr Aldridgs Benedicite Service or his E minor Benedicite (3) | | 52v-53 |
| O God, whose never failing providence | Andreas Hecht | 53 |
| When the Lord turned again the captivity | (Adrian Batten) | 53 |
| O pray for the peace of Jerusalem | Dr Willm Child | 53 |
| Call to remembrance | Richard Farrant | 53v |
| Hide not thou thy face | Richard Farrant | 53v |
| Let my complaint | Adrian Batten | 53v |
| O Lord God of hosts | Willm Turner | 53v-54 |
| The Rest of Mr Aldridg's Service in E minor (5,6,7,8,10) | | 54-54v |

| | | |
|---|---|---|
| Mr Aldridg's Service in Gamut (2,5,6,7,8,10) | | 54v-55 |
| Praise the Lord O my soul (Ps. 146) | Henry Loosmore | 55v |
| *Blessed is the people | Mr Tudway | 55v |
| *Behold, I bring you glad tidings. Xmas Anthem | Henry Purcell | 55v-56 |
| A Second Kyrie & Creed in triple time of Dr Blows in G | | 56v |
| Save me, O God (Ps.54) | Henry Pursel | 56v |
| 'Anthems of 5 & 6 Parts & which are for 2 Means' (heading) | | 57 |
| Save me, O God (Ps.54) | Willm Bird | 57 |
| Deliver me from mine enemies | Robert Parsons | 57 |
| Sing joyfully | Willm Bird | 57v |
| Hosanna to the Son of David | Orlando Gibbons | 57v |
| Lift up your heads | Orlando Gibbons | 58 |
| Lord, who shall dwell in thy tabernacle? | (Adrian Batten) | 58 |
| O clap your hands | Adrian Batten | 58-58v |
| O give thanks (Ps.105) | Willm Tucker | 58v |
| O come let us sing unto the Lord | Robt Ramsey | 58v-59 |
| Why art thou so full of heaviness? | Thos Wilkinson | 59 |
| O Jerusalem, thou that killest the prophets | Thos Wilkinson | 59-59v |
| O clap your hands | Willm Tucker | 59v |
| I will sing unto the Lord | Henry Pursell | 59v-60 |
| O God, wherefore art thou absent? | Mr Blow | 60 |
| The king shall rejoice | John Tomkins | 60 |
| God is our hope and strength (a 8) | John Blow | 60v |
| O clap your hands (Dr Hethers Commencement Song') | Orlando Gibbons | 60v-61 |
| Inclina Domine | (Mr Ramsy) | 61-61v |
| O praise God in his holiness | Willm White | 61v |
| *Mr Purcells Service in B flat (2,4,6,7,8,10) | | 61v-62 |

The number 63, by accident, has not been used in foliation.

f. 64 blank

| | | |
|---|---|---|
| Holy, holy, holy | Adrian Batten | 64v |
| Unto thee, O Lord | Richard Dering | 64v |
| Let God arise | Dr Child | 64v |
| 'Verse Anthems' (heading) | | 65 |
| Almighty God, who by the leading of a star | Dr Bull | 65 |
| Blessed are all they | (Orlando Gibbons) | 65-65v |
| My heart is fixed | Willm Tucker | 65v-66 |
| Sing we merrily | John Blow | 66 |
| I will alway give thanks | Pelham Humfreys, John Blow, and William Turner | 66 |
| I am well pleased | Willm Tucker | 66v |
| Above the stars the Saviour dwells | Dr Christopher Gibbons | 67 |
| Behold I bring you glad tidings | Benjamin Rogers | 67-67v |
| How long wilt thou forget me? | Albertus Bryne | 67v |
| My beloved spake (with an amendment: 'Thus in ye printed books') | Thomas Tomkins | 67v-68 |
| O how amiable are thy dwellings | Mr Loe (?Edward Lowe) | 68 |
| How long wilt thou forget me? (with an amendment: 'Thus in Westminster Books') | Dr Christopher Gibbons | 68v |
| Above the stars the Saviour dwells | Dr Christopher Gibbons | 68v-69 |
| Unto thee I Lord do I lift up | Willm Tucker | 69-69v |
| Lord who shall dwell in thy tabernacle? | Mr Portmans | 69v |
| O Lord, thou hast searched me out | Adrian Batten | 69v-70 |
| I heard a voice in heaven saying, Allelujah | Albertus Bryne | 70-70v |
| Blessed is the man (Ps.1) | Michael Wise | 70v |
| Lord, what is man? | Willm Turner | 70v |
| Lord, let me know mine end | (Matthew Lock) | 70v-71 |

| | | |
|---|---|---|
| Turn thy face from my sins | Matthew Lock | 71 |
| O give thanks (Ps.107) | Will Tucker | 71-71v |
| Wherewithall shall a young man cleanse his ways? | Willm Tucker | 71v |
| God standeth in the congregation | Henry Hall | 72 |
| I was glad | Will Tucker | 72-72v |
| By the waters of Babylon | Michael Wise | 72v-73 |
| Blessed is he that considereth the poor | Michael Wise | 73 |
| The Lord said unto my Lord | Dr Christopher Gibbons | 73v |
| O praise the Lord all ye heathen | Dr Christopher Gibbons | 73v |
| Rejoice in the Lord, O ye righteous | Richard Portman | 74 |
| Not unto us | Matthew Lock | 74 |
| The earth is the Lord's | Dr Child | 74 |
| O be joyful in the Lord | Pelham Humphrey | 74v |
| Blessed are all they | Orlando Gibbons | 74v |
| Almighty God which by the leading of a star | Dr Bull | 74v-75 |
| This is the day | Willm Tucker | 75-75v |
| Haste thee I God | Pellham Humfrys | 75v |
| O Lord our governor | Henry Pursel | 75v-76 |
| By the waters of Babylon | Henry Hall | 76 |
| If ye be risen again | Orlando Gibbons | 76v |
| God be merciful unto us | Dr Christopher Gibbons | 76v-77 |
| Behold, God is my salvation | Thos Tudway | 77 |
| Not unto us O Lord | Matthew Lock | 77-77v |
| Blow ye the trumpet | Henry Pursel | 77v |
| O Lord my God | Pellham Humfrys | 77v |
| 'Anthems of 4 Parts' (heading) | | 78 |
| O pray for the peace of Jerusalem | Dr Willm Child | 78 |
| O Lord rebuke me not | Dr Child | 78 |
| Behold, how good and joyful a thing | Dr Childs | 78-78v |
| Lord I am not highminded | Dr Christopher Gibbons | 78v |

| | | |
|---|---|---|
| Awake my soul, that too securely sleep'st | Mr George Jefferys | 78v |
| Help me, Lord | Dr Christopher Gibbons | 79 |
| Turn thou us, O good Lord | George Jefferys | 79-79v |
| Great and marvellous are thy works | George Jefferys | 79v |
| Turn thee again, O Lord God of hosts | George Jeffrys | 80 |
| How wretched is the state | George Jeffrys | 80-80v |
| O Domine Deus, O amabile | George Jeffrys | 80v |
| O Deus meus | George Jeffrys | 80v-81 |
| Lord, come away | Isaac Blackwell | 81 |
| Have pity upon me, O ye friends | Dr Christopher Gibbons | 81-81v |
| O God, thou art my God | Isaack Blackwell | 81v-82 |
| God is our hope and strength | Silas Taylor | 82-82v |
| Bow down thine ear | Isaack Blackwell | 82v |
| Sing unto the Lord, O ye saints | Dr Christopher Gibbons | 83 |
| Out of the deep | Will Grigory | 83 |
| God be merciful unto us | John Blow | 83v |
| Give the king thy judgments | Mr Henry Alldridge | 83v |
| Give sentence with me | Henry Pursell | 83v |
| *O give thanks. . . and his mercy | (Dr Aldridge) | 84 |
| *Behold now, praise the Lord | Dr Blow | 84 |
| *Have pity upon me, O ye friends (concluded at foot of f.83v) | Mr Wise | 84 |
| *Hear my prayer, O Lord (Ps.102) | Mr Turners | 84v |
| *My God, my God, look upon me | Dr Blow | 84v |
| *I waited patiently | Dr Blow | 85-85v |
| *Try me, O God | Dr Turner | 85v |
| *O God, thou art my God | Mr Purcell | 85v-86 |
| *O sing unto God | Dr Blow | 86 |

| | | |
|---|---|---|
| *O God, thou hast cast us out | Mr Purcell | 87 |
| *Thy word is a lantern (incomplete) | (Mr Purcell) | 87 |
| *O be joyful in God | Dr Blow | 87 |
| *God is our hope and strength (contratenor) | (Dr Aldrich) | 87v |
| *God is our hope and strength (medius) (concluded at foot of f.87) | (Dr Aldrich) | 87v |

## (6) Contratenor Cantoris

Inside front cover: 'W.Gostling' and bookplate. (bookplate also inside back cover)

Fly-leaf


| | |
|---|---|
| A table of all ye Services contained in ys Book | 1 |
| f.1v blank | |
| A Table of all ye Anthems conteined in this Book | 2-4 |
| f.4v blank | |
| Mr Thos Tallis Short Service of 4 parts (1,2,4,6,7,8,10) | 5-7 |
| Mr Nicholas Strogers Short Service (1,2,4,6,7,8,10) | 7-9 |
| Mr Willm Birds short service (1,2,4,6,7,8,10) | 9v-11v |
| Mr Thos Tomkins short service (1,2,4,6,7,8,10) (note on f.13v: 'The difference betw: West. books & mine') | 11v-13v |
| Mr Elway Bevin's short service (1,2,4,6,7,8,10) | 14-16 |
| Mr Orlando Gibbon's short service (1,2,4,6,7,8,10) | 16-18 |
| Mr Albert' Brynes Short Service (2,5,6,7,8,10) | 18-19v |
| Mr Ben Roger's short sharp Service (2,5,6,7,8,10) | 19v-21 |
| Behold now, praise the Lord Benjamin Rogers | 21 |
| Dr Childes sharp Service in D sol re (2,5,8,10,6,7) | 21-23 |
| Dr Childes Service in E minor (2,5,6,7,8,10) | 23-24v |
| Dr Childes Service in F (2,5,6,7,9,11) (note: 'exed: by ye Ks') | 25-26v |
| Mr Richard Farrants high Service (2,4,6,7,8,10) | 26v-28 |
| Mr Portmans short Service (2,4,6,7,8,10) | 28v-30 |
| Mr Thomas Tomkins Service in D sol re (2,5,6,7,8,10) | 30-32 |
| Mr William Mundy's Service of 5 Parts (1,2,4,6,7,8,10) | 32-34 |
| Dr Rogers's Service in Gamut (2,5,6,7,8,10) | 34v-35v |
| Mr Pellam Humfreys Service in E la mi (Decani part) (2,5,6,7,8,10) | 36-37 |
| Mr John Farrants short Service (2,5,6,7, 10) | 37-38 |
| Mr Battens short Service (Decani part) (2,5,6,7,8,10) | 38-39 |
| Dr Rogers's service in E la mi (2,5,6,7,Sanctus, 8,10) | 39-40 |
| Mr Blows Service in G (2,5,8,10) | 40-41 |
| Mr Patricks' Service (2,4,8,10) | 41-41v |

| | | |
|---|---|---|
| Dr Childs Benedicite Service (3,5,6,7,8,10) | | 41v-43 |
| Mr Tuckers Benedicite Service (3,5,6,7,8,10) | | 43-44v |
| Mr Blows Benedicite Service (3,5,6,7,9,11) | | 44v-45v |
| Mr John Amners Cesars Service (2,5,6,7,8,10) | | 46-47v |
| O come hither and hearken ('The Anthem to the foregoing Service') | John Amner | 47v |
| Mr John Amners Service of 4 Parts (2,4,6,7,8,10) | | 48-49v |
| Mr John Farrants Short Service (2,5,6,8,10) (Note: refers back to f.38) | | 49v-50 |
| Mr Adrian Battens short Service (2,5,6,7,8,10) | | 50v-51 |
| The Kyries & Creed to Mr Patricks Service (6,7) | | 51v |
| Mr Joh: Blows Service in A re (2,5,6,7,9,11) | | 51v-52v |
| Mr Wises Morning & Evening Service in D minor (2,5,8,10) | | 52v-53 |
| Dr Childs Te Deum to his Benedicite Service | | 53-53v |
| Dr Childs Service in A re (l.e., A minor) (2,5,6,7,8,10) | | 53v-54 |
| Dr Childs Service in E flatt (2,5,6,7,8,10) | | 54-55 |
| Dr Childs Evening Service with verses in G (9,11) | | 55-55v |
| The Commandments & Creed to Mr Blows Service in G (6,7) (note: 'Its left to ye Tanscriber to side ye Verses') | | 55v |
| Dr Blow's Te Deum to his Benedicite Service | | 56 |
| Mr Alldrigs Service in E la mi (3,5,6,7,8,10) | | 56-57 |
| The Commandments & Creed to Mr Wise's Service in D sol re (6,7) | | 57 |
| Mr John Ferraboscos Evening Service for Verses (8,10) | | 57-57v |
| Mr Aldrigs Service in Gamut (2,5) (note: refers forward to ff.59-59v) | | 57v |
| 'Anthems of 4 voyces' (heading) | | 58 |
| O pray for the peace of Jerusalem | Dr Willm Child | 58 |
| O God, whose never failing providence | Andrew Hecht | 58 |
| When the Lord turned again | Adrian Batten | 58v |
| Call to remembrance | Richard Farrant | 58v |
| Hide not thou thy face | (Richard Farrant) | 58v |
| Let my complaint | Adrian Batten | 59 |
| O Lord God of hosts | Willm Turner | 59 |
| Mr Aldridg's Creed in G | | 59-59v |

| | | |
|---|---|---|
| Mr Aldridg's Evening Service in G (8,10) | | 59v |
| The 2d Creed to Dr Blows Service in G (triple time) | | 59v-60 |
| *Mr Purcells Service in B flat (2,4,6,7,8,10) | | 60-60v |
| ff.61-64v blank | | |
| *O sing unto God | John Blow | 65-65v |
| *O Lord God, to whom vengeance belongeth | J sine nomine B (recte: John Blow?) | 65v |
| *Rogers in A (8,10) | | |
| *My God, my God, look upon me | Dr Blow | 66v |
| *Try me, O God | (Dr Turner) | 66v |
| *I will sing a new song | Mr Wise | 67 |
| O Lord, I have loved the habitation | Tho Tomkins | 67v |
| Save me, O God (Ps.54) | Henry Pursel | 67v |
| 'Full Anthems of 5 Parts' (heading) | | 68 |
| With all our hearts | Thos Tallis | 68 |
| Blessed be thy name | Tho Tallis | 68 |
| O thou God, Almighty Father | Edmund Hooper | 68 |
| O Lord, I bow the knees | Willm Mundy | 68-68v |
| I call and cry | (Thomas Tallis) | 68v |
| Prevent us, O Lord (composer's name cropped in binding) | William Byrd | 68v-69 |
| Behold, it is Christ | Edm Hooper | 69 |
| O Lord, make thy servant Charles | Willm Bird | 69 |
| I lift my heart to thee | Dr Tye | 69-69v |
| O Lord, turn thy wrath (with 2nd part,'Bow thine ear') | Willm Bird | 69v-70 |
| O give thanks | Dr Giles | 70 |
| Almighty God, the fountain of all wisdom | Tho Tomkins | 70-70v |
| Why art thou so full of heaviness? | Thos Wilkinson | 70v |
| O Jerusalem, thou that killest the prophets | Thos Wilkinson | 70v-71 |
| We beseech thee, Almighty God | Adrian Batten | 71 |
| Lord, who shall dwell in thy tabernacle? | Adrian Batten | 71 |

| | | |
|---|---|---|
| 'Full Anthems of 5 or more Parts' (heading) | | 71v |
| Hear my prayer, O God | Adrian Batten | 71v |
| The Lord bless us (note: 'This is to be on Decani side') | Willm White | 71v-72 |
| O come, let us sing unto the Lord | Robt Ramsey | 72 |
| Why art thou so full of heaviness? | Thos Wilkinson | 72 |
| O clap your hands | W.Tucker | 72v |
| I will sing unto the Lord | Henry Pursell | 72v-73 |
| O God, wherefore art thou absent? | Mr Joh: Blow | 73 |
| *Hear my prayer, O Lord (Ps.102) | (Mr Turner) | 73 |
| *Blessed is the man (Psalm 1) | Mr Sargenson | 73-73v |
| *O God, thou art my God (Cantoris) | Mr Purcell | 73v-74 |
| *O God, thou art my God (Decani) | Henry Purcell | 74 |
| Mr Robt Ramsey's Commencement Song of 8 voc: Inclina Domine | | 74v |
| A 8 voc: by Mr Orlando Gibbons O clap your hands (note at end: 'Mr Heathers Commencement Song sett by Mr Gibbons') | | 75 |
| 'Anthems of 6, 7 & 8 parts' (heading) | | 75v |
| The King shall rejoice | John Tomkins | 75v |
| God is our hope and strength (a 8) | Mr Blow | 75v |
| Save me, O God (Ps. 69) | Mr Blow | 76 |
| O praise God in his holiness | Willm White | 76 |
| 'Anthems of 6 or more parts' (heading) | | |
| Sing joyfully | Willm Bird | 76v |
| Deliver me from mine enemies | Rob: Parsons | 76v |
| Hosanna to the Son of David | Orlando Gibbons | 77 |
| Lift up your heads | Orlando Gibbons | 77 |
| O clap your hands | Adrian Batten | 77v |
| *O give thanks (Contratenor I) | Dr Aldrich | 77v |
| *O give thanks (Contratenor II) | Henry Aldrich | 78 |
| *When the Son of Man shall come | Dr Blow | 78-78v |
| Blow up the trumpet | Henry Pursell | 79-79v |
| Not unto us | Matthew Lock | 79v |

| | | |
|---|---|---|
| 'The Second Contratenor of ye vers Anthems'(heading) | | 80 |
| Behold thou hast made my days | Orlando Gibbons | 80 |
| Blessed are all they | Orlando Gibbons | 80 |
| Behold, I bring you glad tidings | Orlando Gibbons | 80-80v |
| How long wilt thou forget me? | Thos Morley | 80v-81 |
| Almighty God, who by the leading of a star (note: part of the composer's name cropped in binding) | Dr Bull | 81 |
| In thee, O Lord, put I my trust | Dr Bull | 81-81v |
| O Lord, let me know mine end | Tho Tomkins | 81v |
| Let God arise | John Ward | 81v |
| Hear my prayer O Lord, hold not thy peace | Thos Wilkinson | 81v-82 |
| Thou art my King, O God | Tho Tomkins | 82 |
| Out of the deep | Thos Morley | 82 |
| I heard a voice in heaven saying, Allelujah | Albert Bryne | 82-82v |
| O praise God in his holiness | Edm Smith (recte Edward) | 82v |
| O how happy a thing it is | Adrian Batten | 82v |
| The earth is the Lords | Willm Turner | 83 |
| O be joyful in God | Willm Turner | 83-83v |
| Blessed is the man(Psalm 1) | Andreas Hecht | 83v-84 |
| Lord, who shall dwell in thy tabernacle? | Andreas Hecht | 84 |
| O come hither and hearken | (John Cutts) | 84v |
| Lord, how long wilt thou be angry? | Wm Tucker | 84v-85 |
| Praise the Lord, ye servants | W.Tucker | 85-85v |
| Lord, who shall dwell in thy tabernacle? | Mr Portman | 85v-86 |
| O Lord, thou hast searched me out | Adrian Batten | 86 |
| How long wilt thou forget me? | Albert Bryne | 86-86v |

| | | |
|---|---|---|
| I heard a voice from heaven saying, Allelujah | Albert Bryne | 86v-87 |
| Belssed is the man (Psalm 1) | Michael Wise | 87 |
| Lord, what is man? | Will Turner | 87-87v |
| Lord, let me know mine end | Matthew Lock | 87v-88 |
| Turn thy face from my sins | Matthew Lock | 88 |
| Behold now, praise the Lord | John Blow | 88 |
| 'Verse Anthems' (heading) | | 88v |
| The Lord said unto my Lord ('The 3d Treble') | Dr Christopher Gibbons | 88v |
| Rejoice in the Lord, O ye righteous | Richard Portman | 88v |
| Not unto us | Matthew Lock | 88v-89 |
| O be joyful in the Lord | Pelham Humfrys | 89 |
| The earth is the Lords | Dr Child | 89v |
| This is the day (note: 'ys Anthem is on Decany side') | Willm Tucker | 89v-90 |
| Comfort ye, my people | Willm Tucker | 89v-90 |
| O Lord our governor | Henry Pursell | 90v |
| I wil alway give thanks | Pellham Humfrys John Blow, Willm Turner | 90v-91 |
| By the waters of Babylon | Henry Hall | 91-91v |
| I will praise the Lord | John Ward | 91v |
| Holy, holy, holy | Adrian Batten | 91v-92 |
| Unto thee, O Lord | Richard Deering | 92 |
| O give thanks (Ps.118) | Pellam Humfrys | 92-92v |
| O Lord, rebuke me not | Dr Child | 92v-93 |
| Behold, how good and joyful a thing | Dr Child | 93 |
| O Lord, my God | P.Humfrys | 93-93v |
| Awake, my soul | George Jeffrys | 93v |
| Help me, Lord | Dr Christopher Gibbons | 93v |
| Turn thou us, O good Lord | George Jeffrys | 93v-94 |
| Great and marvellous | George Jeffrys | 94-94v |
| Turn thee again | George Jeffrys | 94v |
| How wretched is the state | George Jeffrys | 94v-95 |
| Domine Deo, O amabile principia | George Jeffrys | 95 |
| O Deus meus | George Jeffrys | 95-95v |

| | | |
|---|---|---|
| O Lord, come away | Isaac Blackwell | 95v |
| Have pity on me, O ye friends | Dr Christopher Gibbons | 95v-96 |
| O God, thou art my God | Isaac Blackwell | 96 |
| God is our hope and strength | Silas Taylor | 96-96v |
| Bow down thine ear | Isaac Blackwell | 96v-97 |
| Let God arise | Dr Child | 97 |
| Give the King thy judgments | Mr Henry Alldridge | 97 |
| Give sentence with me (note: composer's name added by Gostling) | H.Pursel | 97-97v |
| *Blessed is the people | Mr Tudway | 97v |
| *Behold now, praise the Lord | John Blow | 97v |
| *I was glad | (Mr Purcel) | 97v-98 |
| *I beheld, and lo! a great multitude | Dr Rogers | 98 |
| *O God, thou hast cast us out | Mr Purcell | 98v |
| *Hide not thou thy face | (Aldrich upon Farrant) | 99 |
| *Give sentence with me | (Dr Aldrich) based on O.Gibbons,'Almighty and everlasting God' | 99 |

(7) Tenor Cantoris

Inside front cover: 'W.Gosling' and bookplate (bookplate also inside back cover)
Recipe or prescription in John Gostling's hand: 1

½ pint of sack
of oil of sweet Almons
Ditto oil of Rhow (? rhodium)
for a Clyster probatium (last three letters doubtful)

f.1v blank

A Table of all ye Services contained in ys Book 2

f.2v blank

A Table of all ye Anthems contained in ys Book 3-5

f.5v blank

Mr Thos Tallis short Service (1,2,4,6,7,8) (incomplete) 6-7v

Mr Strogers short Service (1,2,4,6,7,8,10) 8-10

Mr Birds short Service (1,2,4,6,7,8,10) 10-12

Mr Thos Tomkins short Service (1,2,4,6,7,8,10) 12v-14v
(note in (8) with amendment:'so in Westminster books')

Mr Bevins short Service 14v-16v

Mr Orlando Gibbons short Service (1,2,4,6,7,8,10) 16v-18

Mr Albertus Brynes short Service (2,5,6,7,8,10) 18v-19v

Mr Ben Rogers short sharp Service (2,5,6,7,8,10) 20-21

Behold now, praise the Lord (Dr Rogers) 21-21v

Dr Childes sharp Service in D sol re (2,5,8,10) 21v-23

The Keery & Creed of Dr Childs sharp Service in D (6,7) 23-23v

Dr Childes Service in E minor (2,5,6,7,8,10) 23v-24v

Dr Childes Service in F (2,5,6,7,9,11) 24v-26

Mr Richard Farrants high Service (2,4,6,7,8,10) 26-28

Mr Portmans Service (2,4,6,7,8,10) 28-29v

Mr Thomas Tomkins's Service in D minor (2,5,6,7,8,10) 29v-31v

Dr Rogers's Service in Gamut (2,5,6,7,8,10) 31v-32v

Mr Pelham Humfreys Short Service in E la mi (2,5,6,7,8,10) 33-33v

Mr John Farrants short Service (2,5,6,7,8,10) 33v-34v
(note: 'This Service in on Decani side see p.72 (f.41v) for yt on Cantoris side')

Mr Battens short Service (2,5,6,7,8,10) 34v-35v

| | | |
|---|---|---|
| Dr Rogers's Service in E la mi (2,5,6,7,8,10) | | 35v-36v |
| Mr Blows short Service in G (2,5,8,10) | | 36v-37 |
| Mr Patricks Service (2,4,8,10) | | 37v-38 |
| Dr Childs Benedicite Service (3,5,6,7,8,10) | | 38-39 |
| Mr Tuckers Benedicite Service (3,5,6,7,8,10) | | 39-40v |
| Mr Blows Benedicite Service (3,5,6,7,9,11) | | 40v-41 |
| Mr John Farrants short Service (2,4,8) | | 41v-42 |
| Mr Battens short Service (2,5,6,7,8,10) | | 42-43 |
| Mr John Amners Service of 5 Parts called Caesars (2,5,6,7,8,10) | | 43-44v |
| O come hither and hearken | John Amner Organist of Ely | 44v |
| Mr Patricks Commandments & Creed which is to be on Decany side (6,7) | | 44v-45 |
| Mr Blows Service in A re (2,5,6,7,9,11) | | 45-45v |
| Mr Wises Morning & Evening Service with Verses in D minor (2,5,6,8,10) | | 46 |
| The Te Deum to Dr Childs Benedicite Service | | 46v |
| Dr Childs Service in A re (i.e., A minor) (2,5,6,7,8,10) | | 46v-47 |
| Dr Childs flatt Service in E (2,5,6,7,8,10) | | 47-48 |
| Dr Childs Evening Service with verses in Gamut (9,11) | | 48-48v |
| Mr Blows Kyrie & Creed to his Service in G (common time) (6,7) | | 48v |
| Mr Wises Commandments & Creed to his Service in D sol re (6,7) | | 49 |
| Dr Blows Te Deum to his Serice in E la mi | | 49-49v |
| Mr Alldridgs Benedicite Service (3,5,6,7,8,10) | | 49v-50 |
| Mr John Ferabosco's Evening Service in D sol re sharp (8,10) | | 50-51v |
| Mr Alldridg's Service in Gamut (2,5,6,7,8,10) | | 51v-52 |
| Dr Blows Second Commandments & Creed in Gamut (triple time) (6,7) | | 51 |
| *Mr Purcells Service in B flat (2,4,6,7,8,10) | | 51v-52 |
| *Rogers in A re Evening Service (i.e., A minor) (8,10) | | 52v |
| ff.53-55 blank | | |
| 'Of 8 voc' (heading) | | 55v |
| O praise God in his holiness | Willm White | 55v |
| *My God, my God, look upon me | Dr Blow | 55v |
| Mr Robert Ramsys Commencement Song of 8 voc Inclina Domine | | 56 |

| | | |
|---|---|---|
| *Thy way, O God | Mr Purcell | 56 |
| Dr Heathers Commencement Song composed by Mr Orlando Gibbons O clap your hands | | 56v |
| 'Anthems of 4. voyces' (heading) | | 57 |
| O God, whose never failing providence | Andreas Hecht | 57 |
| When the Lord turned again | Adrian Batten | 57 |
| Call to remembrance | Richard Farrant | 57-57v |
| Hide not thou thy face | Richard Farrant | 57v |
| Let my complaint | Adrian Batten | 57v |
| God is our hope (a 8) | Mr Blow | 57v |
| 'Full Anthems of 5 Parts & allso of 6 parts' (heading) | | 58 |
| O come, let us sing unto the Lord | Robert Ramsey | 58 |
| Hosanna to the Son of David | Orlando Gibbons | 58 |
| *When the Son of Man shall come | Dr Blow | 58 |
| O clap your hands | Adrian Batten | 58v |
| Why art thou so full of heaviness? | Thos Wilkinson | 58v |
| O Jerusalem, thou that killest | Thos Wilkinson | 58v-59 |
| Turn thy face from my sins | Matthew Lock | 59-59v |
| I will sing unto the Lord | Henry Pursel | 59v |
| O clap your hands together | Willm Tucker | 59v-60 |
| O God, wherefore art thou absent? | Mr Blow | 60 |
| O Lord, I have loved the habitation | Thomas Tomkins | 60 |
| 'Vers Anthems' (heading) | | 60v |
| Sing unto the Lord, O ye kingdoms | Will Turner | 60v |
| This is the day | Willm Turner | 60v-61 |
| Praise the Lord, O my soul (Ps. 103) | (Mr Hecht) | 61-61v |
| My days are gone | John Cutts | 61v |
| O praise the Lord, ye angels | John Cutts | 61v-62 |
| O sing unto the Lord (Psalm 98) | John Cutts | 62 |
| O sing unto the Lord for it is a good thing | Willm Turner | 62-62v |
| Hear my crying, O God | Andreas Hecht | 62v-64 |

| | | |
|---|---|---|
| By the waters of Babylon | John Cuts | 64-64v |
| Praise the Lord, ye servants (ending on a slip, f.65) | Andreas Hecht | 64v |
| Lord who shall dwell in thy tabernacle? (composer's name cropped in binding) | Andreas Hecht | 64v-66 |
| Haste thee, O God | Andreas Hecht | 66 |
| The earth is the Lord's | Willm Turner | 66v |
| O Lord, thou hast searched me out | Adrian Batten | 66v |
| Lord, how long wilt thou forget me? | Albertus Bryne | 67 |
| I heard a voice from heaven saying, Allelujah | Albertus Bryne | 67 |
| Blessed is the man(Psalm 1) | Mr Wise | 67 |
| Lord, what is man? | Willm Turner | 67v |
| Lord let me know mine end | Matthew Lock | 68 |
| Turn thy face from my sins | Matthew Lock | 67v |
| Lord, how are they increased | John Blow | 68-68v |
| I will cry unto thee, O God | John Blow | 69 |
| Rejoice in the Lord, O ye righteous | Pelham Humfrey | 69 |
| Rejoice in the Lord, O ye righteous | Richard Portman | 69 |
| Not unto us | Matthew Lock | 69v |
| The earth is the Lord's | Dr Child | 69v |
| O be joyful in the Lord | Pelham Humfreys | 69v |
| Blessed are all they that fear the Lord | Orlando Gibbons | 70 |
| Almighty God, who by the leading of a star | Dr Bull | 70 |
| Haste thee, O God | Pellham Humfrys | 70v |
| I am well pleased | Will Tucker | 70v |
| My heart is fixed | Will Tucker | 71 |
| By the waters of Babylon | Mr Henry Hall | 71v-72 |
| Behold, God is my salvation | Mr Tudway | 72-72v |
| O give thanks (Psalm 118) | Mr Pellham Humfrys | 72v |

| | | |
|---|---|---|
| Not unto us (note:'as it is in Mr Tuckers book') | Matthew Lock | 73 |
| Blow up the trumpet | Mr Henry Pursel | 73 |
| Blow up the trumpet (contra tenor) | Henry Pursel | 73 |
| (note: 'The Contratenor & Tenor for ys Anthem are here to sing together') | | |
| O Lord, rebuke me not | Dr Childs | 73v |
| Behold, how good and jouful a thing | Dr Childs | 73v |
| O Lord my God | Mr Pellham Humfrys | 74 |
| Awake my soul, thou too securely sleep'st | George Jeffrys | 74 |
| Help me, Lord | Dr Christopher Gibbons | 74 |
| Turn thou us, O good Lord | George Jeffrys | 74v |
| Great and marvellous are thy works | George Jeffrys | 75 |
| Turn thee again, O Lord God | George Jeffrys | 75-75v |
| How wretched is the state | George Jeffrys | 75v-76 |
| O Domine Deus | George Jeffrys | 76 |
| O Deus meus | George Jeffrys | 76-76v |
| Lord, come away | Isaack Blackwell | 76v |
| Have pity upon me, O ye friends | Dr Christopher Gibbons | 76v-77 |
| O God, thou art my God | Isaack Blackwell | 77-77v |
| God is our hope and strength | Silas Taylor | 77v |
| Bow down thine ear | Isaack Blackwell | 77v-78 |
| Let God arise | Dr Child | 78 |
| O praise the Lord all ye heathen | Henry Pursell | 78v |
| Give the King thy judgments | Mr Henry Alldridge | 78v |
| Give sentence with me | Henry Pursell | 78v-79 |
| *O sing unto the Lord (Psalm 98) | (Dr Child) | 79 |
| *O give thanks ...and his mercy | Dr Aldridge | 79v |
| *Lord, teach us to number our days | Mr Humphreys | 79v-80 |
| *Behold now praise the Lord | Dr Blow | 80 |
| *Have pity upon me, O ye my friends | Mr Wise | 80 |

| | | |
|---|---|---|
| *Hear my prayer, O Lord (Ps. 102) | Mr Turner | 80v |
| *I was glad | (Mr Purcel) | 81 |
| *Hear, O heavens | Pelham Humfrey | 81v |
| *I will alway give thanks | Pelham Humfrey, John Blow, William Turner | 81v-82 |
| *I beheld, and lo! a great multitude | Dr Rogers | 82-82v |
| *I will sing a new song | (Mr Wise) | 82v |
| *Prepare ye the way | Mr Wise | 83 |
| *O praise God in his holiness | Mr Wise | 83v |
| *O clap your hands | Dr Rogers | 83v |
| *O clap your hands (Medius part) | Benjamin Rogers | 84 |
| *The Lord said unto my Lord (also Medius part) | Mr Wise | 84-84v |
| *O give thanks (Psalm 106) | Mr Pursell | 84v-85 |
| *Teach me, O Lord (Medius part) | Christopher Gibbons | 85v |
| *Teach me, O Lord | Dr Christopher Gibbons | 86 |
| *O God, thou art my God | Mr Purcell | 86 |
| *Behold, I bring you glad tidings | Mr Purcell | 86v-87 |
| *Out of the deep | Dr Aldrich | 87 |
| *O praise the Lord, laud ye the name | Dr Child | 87v |
| *I waited patiently | Dr Blow | 87v |
| *Try me, O God | Dr Turner | 88 |
| *O God, thou art my God (Decani part) | Mr Purcell | 88-88v |
| *O God, thou art my God (Cantoris part) | Mr Purcell | 88v |
| *O God, thou hast cast us out (Cantoris with Decani part) | Mr Purcell | 89 |
| *O sing unto God | Dr Blow | 89-89v |
| *Sing we merrily | Dr Blow | 89v-90 |
| *O Lord God, to whom vengeance belongeth | J sine nomine B (recte John Blow?) | 90 |
| *God is our hope and strength | (Dr Aldrich) | 90v |

| | | |
|---|---|---|
| *Hide not thou thy face | R.Farrant(By Dr Aldrich improved) | 91 |
| *Give sentence with me | (Dr Aldrich) based on O.Gibbons, 'Almighty and everlasting God' | 91 |

(8) Bassus Cantoris

Inside front cover: Signature 'W.Gostling' and bookplate
Memorandum:
Munday being 28 April 79 about 1 of ye clock in ye daytime was Mr Airsdens will was open'd in ye presence of ye Principle of Clifforss Inn & me Stephen Bing
Inside back cover: crude note, 'Mr John A. E. (?N)'

| | |
|---|---|
| A table of all ye Anthems contained in ys Book | 1-1v |
| A Table of all ye Services contained in ys Book | 2-3v |
| Mr Thos Tallis's short Service (1,2,4,6,7,8,10) | 4-5v |
| Mr Strogers short Service (1,2,4,6,7,8,10) | 5v-8 |
| Mr Birds short Service (1,2,4,6,7,8,10) (note to (6): 'those notes raced out are so in ye printed books') | 8-9v |
| Mr Thos Tomkins short Service (1,2,4,6,7,8,10) | 9v-12 |
| Mr Bevins short Service (1,2,4,6,7,8,10) | 12-14 |
| Orlando Gibbons short Service (1,2,4,6,7,8,10) | 14-16 |
| Mr Brynes Short Service (2,5,6,7,8,10) | 16-17v |
| Mr Rogers short sharp Service (2,5,6,7,8,10) | 17v-19 |
| Behold now, praise the Lord Ben Rogers | 19 |
| Dr Childes sharp Service in D sol re (2,5,8,10) | 19-20v |
| Dr Childes Kiery & Creed in D sharp | 21 |
| Dr Childes Service in E minor (2,5,6,7,8,10) | 21v-22 |
| Dr Childes Service in F (2,5,6,7,9,11) | 22v-24 |
| Mr Richard Farrants high Service (2,4,6,7,8,10) (between ff.24v and 25 is a small slip containing an omission from Te Deum) | 24-26 |
| Mr Portman's Service (2,4,6,7,8,10) | 26-27v |
| Mr Thomas Tomkins's Service in D minor (2,5,6,7,8,10) | 28-29v |
| Dr Rogers's Service in Gamut (2,5,6,7,8,10) | 29v-31 |
| Mr Pellam Humfreys short Service in E minor (2,5,6,7,8,10) | 31v-32 |
| John Farrants short Service (2,5,6,7,8,10) | 32-33 |
| Mr Battens short Service (2,5,6,7,8,10) | 33-34 |
| Dr Rogers's Service in E la mi (2,5,6,7,8,10) | 34-35 |
| Mr John Blows Service in G (2,5,8,10) | 35-35v |
| Mr Patricks Service (2,4,8,10) | 35v-36 |
| Dr Childs Benedicite Service (3,5,6,7,8,10) | 36v-37v |
| Mr Tuckers Benedicite Service (3,5,6,7) | 37v-38 |
| O come hither and hearken John Cutts | 38v |

| | | |
|---|---|---|
| Tuckers Evening to his Benedicite Service (8,10) | | 39 |
| His (i.e., William Tucker's) short Service (2,5,8,10) | | 39-39v |
| Mr John Amners Caesars Service (2,5,6,7,8,10) | | 40-41 |
| O come hither and hearken | John Amner Organist of Ely | 41 |
| Mr Patricks Kyriee & Creed | | 41-41v |
| Mr Blows Service in A re (2,5,6,7,9,11) | | 41v-42 |
| Mr Wise's Morning & Evening Service for Verses in D minor (2,5,8,10) | | 42v |
| Dr Childs Service in A re (i.e., A minor) (2,5,6,7,8,10) | | 43-43v |
| Dr Childs Service in E flatt (2,5,6,7,8,10) | | 43v-44 |
| Dr Childs Te Deum in Gamut or Benedicite Service | | 44-44v |
| Dr Childs Evening Service in G (9,11) | | 44v |
| Dr Childs Creed to his Service in E flatt (7, also 8,10) | | 45 |
| Dr Childs Te Deum to his Benedicite Service | | 45-45v |
| Mr Blows Benedicite or his Service in E la mi (3,5,6,7,9,11) | | 45v-46v |
| Mr Blows Kyrie & Creed in Gamut | | 46v |
| Mr Wises Commandments & Creed to his Service in D sol re | | 46v-47 |
| Dr Blow's Te Deum to his benedicite Service | | 47 |
| Mr Henry Alldridg's Service in E la mi(3,5,6,7,8,10) | | 47-48 |
| Mr John Ferabosco's Evening Service (8,10) | | 48 |
| Mr Aldridgs Service in Gamut (2,5,6,7,8,10) | | 48-48v |
| Anthems of 5 voyces (heading) | | 49 |
| O come, let us sing unto the Lord | Robert Ramsy | 49 |
| Why art thou so full of heaviness? | Thomas Wilkinson | 49 |
| O Jerusalem, thou that killest the prophets | Mr Wilkinson | 49-49v |
| Turn thy face from my sins | Matthew Locke | 49v |
| I will sing unto the Lord | Henry Pursel | 50 |
| O clap your hands together | Willm Tucker | 50 |
| Save me, O God (Ps. 54) | Henry Pursel | 50v |
| Dr Blows Second Creed in G (triple time) (also 6) | | 50v |
| *The King shall rejoice | John Tomkins | 50v-51 |

| | | |
|---|---|---|
| *Dr Rogers Evening Service in A re (i.e., A minor) (8,10) | | 51 |
| *O God, thou hast cast us out ('Decani') | Mr Purcell | 51v |
| 'Anthems of 4 Parts /& 5' (heading) | | 52 |
| When the Lord turned again | Adrian Batten | 52 |
| O God, whose never failing providence | Andreas Hecht | 52 |
| Call to remembrance | Richard Farrant | 52 |
| Hide not thou thy face | (Richard Farrant) | 52v |
| Let my complaint | Adrian Batten | 52v |
| *Mr Purcels service in B flat (2,4,6,7,8,10) | | 52v-54 |
| *Dr Blow's Te Deum to his E la mi Service | | 54 |
| ff. 54v-62 blank | | |
| *O sing unto God | Dr Blow | 62v-63 |
| *God is our hope and strength | Henry Aldrich | 63 |
| *Hide not thou thy face | Aldrich upon Farrant | 63v |
| *Give sentence with me | Aldrich based on O.Gibbons,'Almighty and everlasting God | 63v |
| ff.64-66 blank | | |
| *I beheld, and lo! a great multitude | Dr Rogers | 66v |
| *I will sing a new song | Mr Wise | 66v-67 |
| Inclina Domine /Mr Robert Ramsy's Commencement Song of 8 voc. | | 67v |
| 'Anthems of 7 voices' (heading) | | 68 |
| O clap your hands | Adrian Batten | 68 |
| God is our hope (a 8) | Mr John Blow | 68 |
| O clap your hands. Dr Heathers Commencement Song composed by Mr Orlando Gibbons | | 68v |
| O praise God in his holiness | Willm White | 69 |
| *How are the mighty fall'n | Mr Wise | 69 |
| *My God, my God, look upon me | Dr Blow | 69v |
| *O God, thou art my God (Dec. and Can.) | Mr Purcell | 69v-70 |
| *Blessed is the man (Ps.1) | John Sargenson | 70v |
| *Try me, O God | Dr Turner | 70v-71 |
| *O God, thou hast cast us out | H. Purcell | 71 |

| | | |
|---|---|---|
| Holy, holy, holy | Adrian Batten | 71v |
| Not unto us | Matthew Lock | 71v |
| *O give thanks ... and his mercy | Mr Aldridge | 71v |
| How long wilt thou forget me? | Albertus Bryne | 72 |
| I heard a voice from heaven saying, Allelujah | Albertus Bryne | 72-72v |
| "Vers Anthems' (heading) | | |
| Blessed is the man (Ps.1) | Mr Wise | 72v-73 |
| Lord, what is man? | Willm Turner | 73 |
| Lord, let me know mine end | Matthew Locke | 73-73v |
| Turn thy face from my sins | Matthew Lock | 73v |
| O Lord, thou hast searched me out | John Blow | 73v-74 |
| Rejoice in the Lord, O ye righteous | Richard Portman | 74 |
| Not unto us | Matthew Lock | 74v |
| The earth is the Lord's | Dr Child | 74v |
| O be joyful in the Lord | Pelham Humfrys | 75 |
| Let God arise | John Ward | 75-75v |
| O Lord our governor | Henry Pursell | 75v-76 |
| My heart is fixed | Wilm Tucker | 76 |
| I will alway give thanks | Pellham Humfrys, John Blow, W.Turner | 76-76v |
| Haste thee, O God | Pellham Humfrys | 76v |
| Sing we merrily | John Blow | 76v |
| I am well pleased | W.Tucker | 76v |
| By the waters of Babylon | Henry Hall | 77 |
| Blow up the trumpet | Henry Purcell | 77v |
| Behold, God is my salvation | Thomas Tudway | 77v |
| O God, wherefore art thou absent? | Mr Blow | 77v-78 |
| Awake, my soul, that too securely sleep'st | George Jeffrys | 78 |
| Help me, Lord | Dr Christopher Gibbons | 78-78v |
| Turn thou us, O good Lord | George Jeffrys | 78v |
| Great and marvellous | George Jeffrys | 78v179 |

| | | |
|---|---|---|
| Turn thee again, O Lord God of hosts | George Jeffrys | 79-79v |
| How wretched is the state | George Jeffrys | 79v |
| O Domine Deus | George Jeffrys | 79v-80 |
| O Deus meus | George Jeffrys | 80 |
| Lord, come away | Isaack Blackwell | 80v |
| Have pity upon me, O ye friends | Dr Christopher Gibbons | 80v |
| O God, thou art my God | Isaac Blackwell | 80v-81 |
| God is our hope and strength | Silas Taylor | 81-81v |
| Bow down thine ear, O Lord | Isaac Blackwell | 81v-82 |
| Let God arise | Dr Childs | 82 |
| Give the King thy judgments | Mr Aldridge | 82-82v |
| Give sentence with me | Henry Pursell | 82v |
| *Praise the Lord, O my soul, while I live | Henry Loosmore | 83 |
| *Have pity upon me, O ye my friends | Mr Wise | 83v |
| *Hear my prayer, O Lord (Ps. 102) | Mr Turner | 83v |
| *Sing unto the Lord, O ye kingdoms | Mr Turner | 84 |

f.84v blank

Index to Catalogue

M - Medius; C-t - Contratenor; T - Tenor; B - Bassus

| | Decani | | | | Cantoris | | | |
|---|---|---|---|---|---|---|---|---|
| | M | C-t | T | B | M | C-t | T | B |
| Anonymous | | | | | | | | |
| Look, shepherds, look | | | 72v | | | | | |
| Aldrich (Henry) 1648-1710 | | | | | | | | |
| 'Benedicite' Service in E minor | 58 | 46v | 103v | 45 | 52v<br>54 | 56 | 49v | 47 |
| Service in G | 58v | 47v | 104v | 45v | 54v | 57v<br>59 | 51v | 48 |
| Give sentence with me (based on O Gibbons, 'Almighty and everlasting God') | 114v | | | | | 99 | 91 | 63v |
| Give the king thy judgments | | | | | 83v | 97 | 78v | 82 |
| God is our hope and strength | 114 | | | | 87v | | 90v | 63 |
| O give thanks ...and his mercy | 71 | 57 | | | 84 | 77v<br>78 | 79v | 71v |
| Out of the deep | 38v | 61 | | 58v | | | 87 | |
| See also R.Farrant | | | | | | | | |
| Amner (John) 1579-1641 | | | | | | | | |
| 'Caesar's'Service in G | 46v | 38v | 40v | 35 | 43v | 46 | 43 | 40 |
| Short, or Third Service | 48v | | 42v | 36v | | 48 | | |
| O come hither, and hearken | 48 | 40 | 42v | 36v | 45 | 47v | 44v | 41 |
| Batten (Adrian) 1591-1637 | | | | | | | | |
| Short Service | 34v | 31v | 35 | 30 | 36 | 38<br>50v | 34v<br>42 | 33 |
| Christ rising again | | 84v | 84 | | | | | |
| Deliver us, O Lord | 45 | 54v | 54 | 53v | | | | |
| Haste thee, O God (with 2nd part, But let all those that seek thee) | 41v | 53v | 52v | 52v | | | | |

| | Decani | | | | Cantoris | | | |
|---|---|---|---|---|---|---|---|---|
| | M | C-t | T | B | M | C-t | T | B |
| Hear my prayer, O God | 101v | 70v | 60 | 67 | | 71v | | |
| Hide not thou thy face | 41 | 53 | 52 | 67v<br>52 | | | | |
| Holy, holy, holy | 87 | 77v | 68~~v~~ | 81 | 64v | 91v | | 71v |
| Let my complaint come before thee | 62 | 56v | 56v | 54v | 53v | 59 | 57v | 52v |
| Lord, we beseech thee give ear | 41v | 53 | 52v | 52v | | | | |
| Lord, who shall dwell in thy tabernacle? | 76 | 70v | 63 | 77 | 58 | 71 | | |
| My soul truly waiteth | 45 | 54v | 54 | 53v | | | | |
| O clap your hands | 76 | 71 | 63v | 76v | 58 | 77v | 58v | 68 |
| O how happy a thing it is | 94v | 84 | 82 | | | 82v | | |
| O Lord our governor | 95 | 85 | 79 | 99v | | | | |
| O Lord, thou hast searched me out | 101v | | | 77 | 69v | 86 | 66v | |
| O praise the Lord, all ye heathen | 40v | 53 | 52 | 52 | | | | |
| O sing joyfully | 45v | 55 | 54v | 53v | | | | |
| Out of the deep (Daniel & Le Huray, Version I) | 88v | 91v | 78 | 80v | | | | |
| We beseech thee, Almighty God | 69 | 70v | 60v | 67 | | 71 | | |
| When the Lord turned again the captivity | 41v | 53v | 52v | 52v | 53 | 58v | 57 | 52 |
| Bevin (Elway) c1554-1638 | | | | | | | | |
| Short, or First Service | 11v | 12 | 14 | 11 | 12 | 14 | 14v | 12 |
| Blackwell (Isaac) fl1674-87 | | | | | | | | |
| Bow down thine ear | | | | | 82v | 96v | 77v | 81v |
| Lord, come away | | | | | 81 | 95v | 76v | 80v |
| O God, thou art my God | | | | | 81v | 96 | 77 | 80v |

| | Decani | | | | Cantoris | | | |
|---|---|---|---|---|---|---|---|---|
| | M | C-t | T | B | M | C-t | T | B |
| Blow (John) 1649-1708 | | | | | | | | |
| Service in A | 50v | 40v | 44v | 38v | 45v | 51v | 45 | 41v |
| 'Benedicite' Service in E minor | 54v | 37 | 48 | 42 | 50 | 44v | 40v | 45v<br>47v |
| Te Deum to Service in E minor | 57<br>63 | 46v | 103 | 44v<br>48 | 52 | 56 | 49 | 47<br>54 |
| Morning and Evening Service in C | 36v | 33v | 37 | 31v | 38 | 40 | 36v | 35 |
| Communion Service in G | 56v | 44v | 47v | 43v | 51 | 55v | 48v | 46v |
| Second Communion Service in G, triple time | 59v | 48v | 49v | 46v | 56v | 59v | 51 | 50v |
| Behold, how good and joyful a thing | 104v | 94v | 88 | 88 | | | | |
| Behold now, praise the Lord | 81 | | | | 84 | 88<br>97v | 80 | |
| Christ being raised from the dead | 106v<br>107<br>110v | 97<br>102v | 90v<br>95v | 90<br>99 | | | | |
| God be merciful unto us | 112v | 107v | 101 | 107v | 83v | | | |
| God is our hope and strength (a 8) | 76v | 76v | 68v | 75v | 60v | 75v | 57v | 68 |
| I waited patiently | 73 | 62 | | 71 | 85 | | 87v | |
| I will cry unto thee, O God | 105 | 95 | 88v | 88v | | | 69 | |
| Lord, how are they increased | 104 | 94v | 87v | 95 | | | 68 | |
| My God, my God, look upon me | | | | | 84v | 66v | 55v | 69v |
| O be joyful in God | | 62v | | 71v | 87 | | | |
| O God, wherefore art thou absent? | 70 | 76v | 100 | 104v | 60 | 73 | 60 | 77v |
| O how amiable are thy dwellings | 79v | 104v | 98v | 102 | | | | |
| O Lord God to whom vengeance belongeth | 113v | | | 59 | | 65v | 90 | |
| O Lord, I have sinned | 110 | 102 | 95v | 98v | | | | |
| O Lord, thou hast searched me out | 80<br>86v | 97v | 91v | 90v | | | | 73v |
| O sing unto God | | | | | 86 | 65 | 89v | 62v |

| | Decani | | | | Cantoris | | | |
|---|---|---|---|---|---|---|---|---|
| | M | C-t | T | B | M | C-t | T | B |
| Save me, O God (Ps.69) | 70v | 77 | 61v | 105 | | 76 | | |
| Sing we merrily | 86v | 100v | 94 | 97 | 66 | | 89v | 76v |
| The Lord hear thee | 62v | 57 | 56 | 55v | | | | |
| Turn thee unto me | 105v | 95v<br>99v | 89v | 88v | | | | |
| When the Son of Man shall come | 113v | | | 71 | | 78 | 58 | |
| Bryne/Bryan (Albertus) c1621-1671 | | | | | | | | |
| Short Service in G | 15v | 15v | 17 | 14v | 18 | 18 | 18v | 16 |
| How long wilt thou forget me? | 92 | 83v | 80v | 85v | 67v | 86 | 67 | 72 |
| I heard a voice in heaven saying, Allelujah | 102 | 82v | 73 | 86 | 70 | 82<br>86v | 67 | 72 |
| Bull (John) ?1562 or 3 - 1628 | | | | | | | | |
| Almighty God, which by the leading of a star | 90 | 79 | 74v<br>108v | 84 | 65<br>74v | 81 | 70 | |
| In thee, O Lord, put I my trust | 90 | 79 | 69 | 84 | | 81 | | |
| Byrd/Bird (William) 1543 - 1623 | | | | | | | | |
| Short Service | 8 | 8v | 10v | 7v | 10 | 9v | 10 | 8 |
| O Lord, make thy servant Charles | 66 | 68 | 58 | 65 | | 69 | | |
| O Lord, turn thy wrath (with 2nd part, Bow thine ear) | 66v | 68v | 58v | 65v | | 69v | | |
| Prevent us, O Lord | 65v | 67v | 57v | 64v | | 68v | | |
| Save me, O God (Ps.54) | 68v | 70 | 69<br>82v | 67 | 57 | | | |
| Sing joyfully | 75 | 75v | 63 | 76 | 57v | 76v | | |

| | Decani | | | | Cantoris | | | |
|---|---|---|---|---|---|---|---|---|
| | M | C-t | T | B | M | C-t | T | B |
| Child (William) 1606 or 7 - 1697 | | | | | | | | |
| Service in A minor | 52 | 42 | 46 | 40 | 47v | 53v | 46v | 43 |
| Service in D | 18v | 17v | 19v | 17 | 21v | 21 | 21v | 19 |
| Service in E minor | 20v | 19v<br>45 | 21 | 18v | 23 | 23 | 23v | 21v |
| 'Flat' Service in E | 53 | 43 | 107v | 40v | 48v | 54 | 47 | 43v<br>45 |
| Service in F | 23 | 20v | 22 | 19v | 25 | 25 | 24v | 22v |
| 'Benedicite' Service in G | 38 | 35 | 38v | 33 | 40 | 41v | 38 | 36v |
| Service in G, alternative Canticles | 54 | 43v | 47 | 41v | 47v<br>49 | 53<br>55 | 46v<br>48 | 44<br>45 |
| Behold, how good and joyful a thing | 111 | 107v | 100v | 106 | 78 | 93 | 73v | |
| If the Lord himself | 46 | 55v | 55 | 54v | | | | |
| Let God arise | 111v | 107 | 100v | 106v | 64v | 97 | 78 | 82 |
| O clap your hands | 45v | 55v | 54v | 54v | | | | |
| O Lord, grant the king a long life | 45v | 55v | 55 | 54 | | | | |
| O Lord, rebuke me not (Daniels & le Huray, Version I) | | | 100v | 105v | 78 | 92v | 73v | |
| O praise the Lord (Ps. 135) | 72v<br>74v | 61v | | 58v | | | 87v | |
| O pray for the peace of Jerusalem | 46 | 56 | 54v | 55 | 53<br>78 | 58 | | |
| O sing unto the Lord (Ps. 98) | 75<br>78 | 108v | | 109 | | | 79 | |
| Praise the Lord, O my soul (Ps.103) | 45 | 55 | 55v | 54 | | | | |
| The earth is the Lord's | | 99v | 92 | 92 | 74 | 89v | 69v | 74v |
| Thou art my king, O God | 112v | 107v | 101 | 107v | | | | |

| | Decani | | | | Cantoris | | | |
|---|---|---|---|---|---|---|---|---|
| | M | C-t | T | B | M | C-t | T | B |
| Cranford (William) c1650-1675 | | | | | | | | |
| O Lord, make thy servant Charles | 93v | 82 | 76 | 93 | | | | |
| Cutts (John) *1691 or 2 | | | | | | | | |
| By the waters of Babylon | 83 | 86 | 71v | | | | 64 | |
| I give you a new commandment | 42v | 54v | 53 | 53 | | | | |
| I will give thanks (Ps.138) | 100 | 92 | 84v | | | | | |
| I will magnify thee | 94v | 85 | 77 | | | | | |
| Let thy merciful ears | | | 54 | | | | | |
| My days are gone | 84v | 87v | 71 | | | | 61v | |
| O come hither and hearken | 100v | | 85 | 85 | | 84v | | 38v |
| O praise the Lord, ye angels | 85 | 87v | 71 | | | | 61v | |
| O sing unto the Lord (Ps. 98) | 85v | 88 | 71 | | | | 62 | |
| Dering (Richard) c1580 - 1630 | | | | | | | | |
| Unto thee, O Lord, will I lift up | 87 | 77v | 68v | 81 | 64v | 92 | | |
| Farrant (John) fl pre-Civil War | | | | | | | | |
| Short Service | 33v | 31 | 34v | 29v | 35v | 37<br>49v | 33v<br>41v | 32 |
| Farrant (Richard) *1581 | | | | | | | | |
| 'High' Service in A minor | 24 | 22 | 23v | 21 | 26v | 26v | 26 | 24 |
| Call to remembrance | 39 | 51v | 50v | 50v | 53v | 58v | 57 | 52 |
| Hide not thou thy face | 39v | 51v | 50v | 50v | 53v | 58v | 57v | 52v |
| -ditto- adapted by Aldrich | 114 | | | | | 99 | 91 | 63v |

| | Decani | | | | Cantoris | | | |
|---|---|---|---|---|---|---|---|---|
| | M | C-t | T | B | M | C-t | T | B |
| Ferrabosco (John) 1626-1682 | | | | | | | | |
| Verse Evening Service | 57v | 47v | 104 | 45v | 52v | 57 | 50 | 48 |
| Gibbons (Christopher) 1615-1676 | | | | | | | | |
| Above the stars the Saviour dwells | 95v | 85v | 70v | 93v | 67<br>68v | | | |
| God be merciful unto us | 110v | 105 | 100 | 105 | 76v | | | |
| Have pity upon me, O ye friends | | | | | 81 | 95v | 76v | 80v |
| Help me, Lord | | | | | 79 | 93v | 74 | 78 |
| How long wilt thou forget me? | 92v | 85v | 83 | 94 | 68v | | | |
| Lord, I am not highminded | 111v | 78v | 68 | 106v | 78v | | | |
| O praise the Lord, all ye heathen | 108 | 101v | 95 | 98 | 73v | | | |
| Sing unto the Lord, O ye saints | 112 | 107 | | 107 | 83 | | | |
| Teach me, O Lord | 82v | 60 | | 78 | | | 85v<br>86 | |
| The Lord said unto my Lord | 107v | 101v | 91 | 90v | 73v | 88v | | |
| Gibbons (Orlando) 1583 - 1625 | | | | | | | | |
| Short Service | 14 | 13v | 15v | 13v | 16 | 16 | 16v | 14 |
| Almighty and everlasting God | 40v | 52v | 51v | 51v | | | | |
| Behold, I bring you glad tidings | 91 | 79v | 73 | 81v | | 80 | | |
| Behold, thou hast made my days | 90v | 79v | 75 | 84 | | 80 | | |
| Blessed are all they | 90v | 79v | 75v | 84v | 65<br>74v | 80 | 70 | |
| Deliver us, O Lord (with 2nd part, Blessed be the Lord God) | 41 | 53 | 52 | 52 | | | | |

| | Decani | | | | Cantoris | | | |
|---|---|---|---|---|---|---|---|---|
| | M | C-t | T | B | M | C-t | T | B |
| Glorious and powerful God | 91 | 80 | 78v | 81v | | | | |
| Hosanna to the Son of David | 75v | 76 | 63v | 76 | 57v | 77 | 58 | |
| If ye be risen again with Christ | 91v | 80v | 83 | 81v | 76v | | | |
| Lift up your heads | 75v | 76 | 64 | 76v | 58 | 77 | | |
| O clap your hands (with 2nd part 'God is gone up') | 76v | 75 | 64v | 75 | 60v | 75 | 56v | 68v |
| See also Aldrich | | | | | | | | |
| Giles (Nathaniel) c1558 - 1634 | | | | | | | | |
| O give thanks (eclectic text) | 67 | 69 | 59 | 65v | | 70 | | |
| Gregory (William fl 1651 - 1687 | | | | | | | | |
| O God, thou hast cast us out | 113 | 107v | 101 | 108 | | | | |
| Out of the deep | 112 | 107 | 101 | 107 | 83 | | | |
| Hall Henry c1656 - 1707 | | | | | | | | |
| By the waters of Babylon | | 102v | | | 76 | 91 | 71v | 77 |
| God standeth in the congregation | 104v | 95 | 88v | 88v | 72 | | | |
| Heardson (Thomas) | | | | | | | | |
| Almighty God, we beseech thee, give ear | 38v | 51 | 50 | 50 | | | | |
| Keep, we beseech thee, O good Lord | 39 | 51v | 50v | 50v | | | | |
| Hecht (Andreas) | | | | | | | | |
| Blessed is the man (Ps.1) | 84 | 86v | 74 | | | 83v | | |
| Haste thee, O God | 85 | 90 | 72 | 82v | | | 66 | |
| Hear my crying, O God | 83<br>98v | 90v | 71v | 83v | | | 62v | |

| | Decani | | | | Cantoris | | | |
|---|---|---|---|---|---|---|---|---|
| | M | C-t | T | B | M | C-t | T | B |
| Lord, who shall dwell in thy tabernacle? | 84v | 92 | 72 | | | 84 | 64v | |
| O God, whose neverfailing providence | 42 | 53v | 53<br>69 | 53 | 53 | 58 | 57 | 52 |
| Praise the Lord, O my soul (Ps.103) | 84v | | 70v | | | | 61 | |
| Praise the Lord, ye servants | 83 | 78v | 71v | 83 | | | 64v | |
| Henstridge (Daniel) c1646 - 1737 | | | | | | | | |
| Verse Service | 59v | | | | | | | |
| Hooper (Edmund) c1553 - 1621 | | | | | | | | |
| Behold, it is Christ | 66 | 68 | 58 | 65 | | 69 | | |
| O thou God, Almighty Father | 65 | 67 | 57 | 64 | | 68 | | |
| Teach me thy way | 40v | 52v | 51v | 51v | | | | |
| Humfrey (Pelham) 1647 - 1674 | | | | | | | | |
| Short Service in E minor | 32v | 30 | 33v | 29 | 34 | 36 | 33 | 31v |
| By the waters of Babylon | 87v | 103 | 96v | 99v | | | | |
| Haste thee, O God | | 99 | 93<br>94v | 95 | 75v | | 70v | 76v |
| Have mercy upon me (Musica Britannica, vol. 34, version II) | 110 | 101v | 95 | 98 | | | | |
| Hear, O heavens | 79v | 105v | 98 | 102 | | | 81v | |
| Like as the hart | 80v | 105 | 99v | 104 | | | | |
| Lord, teach us to number our days | 80 | 106 | 99 | 103 | | | 79v | |
| O be joyful in the Lord | | 99 | | 92 | 74v | 89 | 69v | 75 |
| O give thanks (Ps. 118) | 80 | 106 | 99v<br>105 | 103v | | 92 | 72v | |

| | Decani | | | | Cantoris | | | |
|---|---|---|---|---|---|---|---|---|
| | M | C-t | T | B | M | C-t | T | B |
| O Lord, my God | | 106v | 100v | 106 | 77v | 93 | 74 | |
| Rejoice in the Lord, O ye righteous | 106 | 95v | 89v | 89 | | | 69 | |
| (with John Blow and William Turner: I will alway give thanks) | 81v | 101 | 94v | 97 | 66 | 90v | 81v | 76 |
| Jeffreys (George) c1610 - 1685 | | | | | | | | |
| Awake, my soul, that too securely sleep'st | | | | | 78v | 93v | 74 | 78 |
| Great and marvellous are thy works | | | | | 79v | 94 | 75 | 78v |
| How wretched is the state | | | | | 80 | 94v | 75v | 79v |
| O Domine Deus (with 2nd part, O Deus meus) | | | | | 80v | 95 | 76 | 79v |
| Turn thee again, O Lord God of hosts | | | | | 80 | 94v | 75 | 79 |
| Turn thou us, O good Lord | | | | | 79 | 93v | 74v | 78v |
| King (William) 1624 - 1680 | | | | | | | | |
| Now that the Lord hath re-advanced the crown | 93v | 83 | 78 | | | | | |
| O sing unto the Lord (Ps. 149) | | | 84v | | | | | |
| Lawes (Henry) 1596 - 1662 | | | | | | | | |
| My song shall be of mercy | 93v | 83 | 77v | 93v | | | | |
| Zadok the priest | 42 | 54 | 83 | 53 | | | | |
| Lawes (William) 1602 - 1645 | | | | | | | | |
| Let God arise | 87v | 103v | 97 | 100v | | | | |
| The Lord is my light | 98 | 92v | 85 | 84v | | | | |
| Locke (Matthew) 1621 or 2 - 1677 | | | | | | | | |
| Lord, let me know mine end | 102v | 93v | 86v | 77v | 70v | 87v | 68 | 73 |

| | Decani | | | | Cantoris | | | |
|---|---|---|---|---|---|---|---|---|
| | M | C-t | T | B | M | C-t | T | B |
| Not unto us (Musica Britannica vol. 38, "A") | 108v | 98 | 91v | 91v | 74 | 88v | 69v | 74v |
| Not unto us (Musica Britannica vol. 38, "B") | 87v | 103 | 97 | 100 | 77 | 79v | 73 | 71v |
| Turn thy face from my sins | 103 | 71v | 87 | 87v | 71 | 88 | 59<br>67v | 49v<br>73v |
| Loosemore (George) *1682 | | | | | | | | |
| O that mine eyes would melt | 96v | | 73v | | | | | |
| Loosemore (Henry) *1670 | | | | | | | | |
| Let all the world in every corner sing | 94 | 83v | 82 | | | | | |
| Praise the Lord, O my soul (Ps.146) | | 73v | 68 | | 55v | | | 83 |
| Lowe (Edward) c1610 - 1682 | | | | | | | | |
| O how amiable are thy dwellings | 94 | | 80v | | 68 | | | |
| Morley (Thomas) 1557 or 8 - 1602 | | | | | | | | |
| How long wilt thou forget me? | 92 | 81 | 83v | | | 80v | | |
| Out of the deep | 91v | 80v | 74v | 80v | | 82 | | |
| Mundy (William) c1529 - ?1591 | | | | | | | | |
| Service in D minor | 28v | 26v | 29 | 25v | | 32 | | |
| O Lord, I bow the knees of my heart | 65 | 67 | 57 | 64v | | 68 | | |
| O Lord, the maker of all things | 40 | 52 | 51 | 51 | | | | |
| O Lord, the world's Saviour | 40 | 52v | 51v | 51v | | | | |
| Parsons (Robert) c1530 - 1570 | | | | | | | | |
| Deliver me from mine enemies | 75 | 75v | 63 | 76 | 57 | 76v | | |

| | Decani | | | | Cantoris | | | |
|---|---|---|---|---|---|---|---|---|
| | M | C-t | T | B | M | C-t | T | B |
| Patrick (Nathaniel) *1595 | | | | | | | | |
| Morning and Evening Service in G minor | 37 | 34 | 38 | 32 | 39v | 41 | 37v | 35v |
| Communion Service in G minor | 50 | 40v | 44 | 38 | 45 | 51v | 44v | 41 |
| Peerson (Martin) 1571/3 - 1651 | | | | | | | | |
| Blow out the trumpet | 42 | 54 | 53 | 52v | | | | |
| Portman (Richard) *c1655 | | | | | | | | |
| Service in G | 26 | 23v | 25 | 23 | 29v | 28v | 28 | 26 |
| Lord, who shall dwell in thy tabernacle? | 100v | 92v | 86 | 86 | 69v | 85v | | |
| Rejoice in the Lord, O ye righteous | 108v | 97v | 91v | 91v | 74 | 88v | 69 | 74 |
| Purcell (Henry) 1659 - 1695 | | | | | | | | |
| Service in B flat | 60v | 48v | 62 | 46v | 61v | 60 | 51v | 52v |
| Behold, I bring you glad tidings | | 60v | | 57v | 55v | | 86v | |
| Blessed be the Lord my strength | 79v | 105 | 98 | 101v | | | | |
| Blow up the trumpet | 87v | 103v | 97 | 101 | 77v | 79 | 73 | 77v |
| Give sentence with me | | | | | 83v | 97 | 78v | 82v |
| I was glad | 113 | | | 55v | | 97v | 81 | |
| I will sing unto the Lord | 69v | 72 | 61 | 68v | 59v | 72v | 59v | 50 |
| Let God arise | 111 | 104 | 97v | 101v | | | | |
| O give thanks (Ps,106) | 82 | 59 | | 56v | | | 84v | |
| O God, the king of glory | 62v | 56v | 56 | 55v | | | | |
| O God, thou art my God | | | | | 85v | 74 | 86<br>88 | 69v |
| O God, thou hast cast us out | | | | | 86v | 98v | 89 | 51v<br>71 |

| | Decani | | | | Cantoris | | | |
|---|---|---|---|---|---|---|---|---|
| | M | C-t | T | B | M | C-t | T | B |
| O Lord our governor | 109v | 100 | 93v | 96 | 75v | 90v | | 75v |
| O praise the Lord, all ye heathen | 113 | 108 | 102 | 108v | | | 78v | |
| Save me, O God (Ps.54) | 70v | 73 | 61v | 68v | 56v | 67v | | 50v |
| Thy way, O God, is holy | 79 | 58 | | 70 | | | 56 | |
| Thy word is a lantern | | 64v | | 72v | 87 | | | |
| Ramsey (Robert) fl c1612 - 1644 | | | | | | | | |
| Inclina, Domine | 77 | 74v | 65 | 74v | 61 | 74v | 56 | 67v |
| O come, let us sing unto the Lord | 67v | 69 | 59v | 66 | 58v | 72 | 58 | 49 |
| Read (-?-) ? - ? | | | | | | | | |
| Evening Service | | | 28v | | | | | |
| Rogers (Benjamin) 1614 - 1698 | | | | | | | | |
| Evening Service in A minor | 72v | | | | | 66 | 52v | 51 |
| Short Service in D | 16v | 16v | 18v | 16 | 19v | 19v | 20 | 17v |
| Service in E minor | 35v | 32v | 36 | 31 | 37<br>38v | 39 | 35v | 34 |
| Service in G | 31v | 29 | 32 | 27v | 32v | 34v | 31v | 29v |
| Behold, I bring you glad tidings | 96 | 86 | 70 | | 67 | | | |
| Behold now, praise the Lord | 18 | 17v | 19v | 17 | 21 | 21 | 21 | 19 |
| I beheld, and lo! a great multitude | 71v | | | | | 98 | 82 | 66v |
| O clap your hands | 78v | 57v<br>58 | | 69v | | | 83v<br>84 | |
| O give thanks (Ps. 107) | 96v | | 53v | | | | | |
| Teach me, O Lord | 62 | 56 | 56 | 55 | | | | |

| | Decani | | | | Cantoris | | | |
|---|---|---|---|---|---|---|---|---|
| | M | C-t | T | B | M | C-t | T | B |
| Sargenson (John) ? - ? | | | | | | | | |
| Blessed is the man (Ps.1) | 72 | | 65v | | | 73 | | 70v |
| Smith (Edward) ? -*1612 | | | | | | | | |
| O praise God in his holiness | | 82v | 81v | | | 82v | | |
| Strogers (Nicholas) fl 1560 - 1575 | | | | | | | | |
| Short Service | 6v | 6v | 8v | 5v | 7v | 7 | 8 | 5v |
| O God, be merciful unto us | 38v | 51 | 50 | 50 | | | | |
| Tallis (Thomas) c1505 - 1585 | | | | | | | | |
| Short Service | 5 | 5 | 7 | 4 | 6 | 5 | 6 | 4 |
| Blessed be thy name, O God | 65 | 67 | 107<br>57 | 64 | | 68 | | |
| I call and cry | 65 | 67v | 57v | 64 | | 68v | | |
| O Lord, give thy holy spirit | 38v | 51 | 50 | 50 | | | | |
| With all our hearts | 65 | 67 | 57 | 64 | | 68 | | |
| Taylor (Silas) 1624 - 1678 | | | | | | | | |
| God is our hope and strength | | | | | 82 | 96 | 77v | 81 |
| Tomkins (John) 1586 - 1638 | | | | | | | | |
| The king shall rejoice | 70 | 76v | 64 | 75v | 60 | 75v | | 50v |
| Tomkins (Thomas) 1572 - 1656 | | | | | | | | |
| Short Service in C | 10 | 10v | 12v | 9v | 14 | 11v | 12v | 9v |
| Second Service in D minor | 27v | 24v | 26v | 24 | 31 | 30 | 29v | 28 |
| Almighty God, the fountain of all wisdom | 68 | 70 | 60 | 66v | | 70 | | |

| | Decani | | | | Cantoris | | | |
|---|---|---|---|---|---|---|---|---|
| | M | C-t | T | B | M | C-t | T | B |
| My beloved spake | 93 | 84 | 79v | 78 | 67v | | | |
| O Lord, I have loved the habitation | 70 | 73 | | 68v | | 67v | 60 | |
| O Lord, let me know mine end | | 81 | 75v | | | 81v | | |
| Thou art my king, O God | 93 | 82 | 79 | | | 82 | | |
| Tucker (William) *1679 | | | | | | | | |
| Short Service in D minor | 44 | | | 34v | 42v | | | 39 |
| 'Benedicite' Service in F | 42v | 36 | 39v | 33v | 41 | 43 | 39 | 37v<br>39 |
| Comfort ye, my people | 83v<br>100 | 101 | 72 | 95v | | 90 | | |
| I am well pleased | | 100v | 93v | 97v | 66v | | 70v | 76v |
| I was glad | 106 | 96 | 90v | 89v | 72 | | | |
| I will magnify thee | 106 | 96 | 90 | 89 | | | | |
| Lord, how long wilt thou be angry? | 101 | 99 | 85v | 85v | | 84v | | |
| My heart is fixed | | 100v | 94 | 96v | 65v | | 71 | 76 |
| O clap your hands | 69v | 72 | 61 | 68 | 59v | 72v | 59v | 50 |
| O give thanks (Ps. 105) | 44v<br>69 | 71 | 55v | 55<br>67v | 58v | | | |
| O give thanks (Ps. 107) | 103v | 94 | 87v | 87v | 71 | | | |
| Praise the Lord, ye servants | 100v | 101v | 85v | 85v | | 85 | | |
| This is the day | 109 | 98v | 93 | 94v | 75 | 89v | | |
| Unto thee, O Lord, do I lift up | 95 | 85 | 69v | 83v | 69 | | | |
| Wherewithal shall a young man cleanse? | 104 | 94 | 88 | 88 | 71v | | | |
| Tudway (Thomas) c1650 - 1726 | | | | | | | | |
| Behold, God is my salvation | 79v | 78 | 99 | 103 | 77 | | 72 | 77v |

| | Decani | | | | Cantoris | | | |
|---|---|---|---|---|---|---|---|---|
| | M | C-t | T | B | M | C-t | T | B |
| Blessed is the people | | | | | 55v | 97v | | |
| My God, my God, look upon me | 109 | 98 | 92v | 94 | | | | |
| Turner (William) 1651 - 1740 | | | | | | | | |
| Behold, God is my salvation | 86 | 87 | 96 | 82 | | | | |
| Behold, how good and joyful a thing | 85 | 54v | 53v | | | | | |
| By the waters of Babylon | 86v | 91 | 84 | | | | | |
| Hear my prayer, O Lord (Ps. 102) | 81 | 73<br>74 | | | 84v | 73 | 80v | 83v |
| Lord, thou hast been our refuge | 79v | 105v | 98v | 102v | | | | |
| Lord, what is man? | 102v | 93 | 86v | 87 | 70v | 87 | 67v | 73 |
| O be joyful in God | 84 | 88v | 88v | | | 83 | | |
| O Lord God of hosts | 62 | 72v | 56v | 104v | 53v | 59 | | |
| O praise the Lord (Ps. 147) | 83<br>86 | 91 | 71v | | | | | |
| O sing unto the Lord for it is a good thing | | | | | | | 6? | |
| Sing, O daughter of Zion | 42v<br>85v | 54 | 53v | 53v | | | | |
| Sing unto the Lord, O ye kingdoms | 83v | 90 | 70 | | | | 60v | 84 |
| The earth is the Lord's | 83v | 86<br>89 | 83v | | | 83 | 66v | |
| This is the day | 84 | 89v | 70 | | | | 60v | |
| Try me, O God | 113v | 62 | 66 | 58 | 85v | 66v | 88 | 70v |
| Tye (Christopher) c1505 - ?1572 | | | | | | | | |
| I lift my heart to thee | 66v | 68 | 58v | 65 | | 69 | | |
| I will exalt thee (with 2nd part, Sing unto the Lord) | 39v | 51v | 50v | 50v | | | | |

| | Decani | | | | Cantoris | | | |
|---|---|---|---|---|---|---|---|---|
| | M | C-t | T | B | M | C-t | T | B |
| Ward (John) 1571 - c1638 | | | | | | | | |
| Bow down thine ear | 94v | 84v | 76v | | | | | |
| I will magnify thee (See Cutts above) | | | | | | | | |
| I will praise the Lord | 88v | 78 | 80 | 80v | | 91v | | |
| Let God arise | 98 | 81v | 81 | 92v | | 81v | | 75 |
| Weelkes (Thomas) *1623 | | | | | | | | |
| O Lord, grant the king a long life | | | | 76v | | | | |
| White (Robert) c1538 - 1574 or (William) c1585 - 1625 | | | | | | | | |
| The Lord bless us (?Robert) | 68v | 71v | 60v | 68 | | 71v | | |
| O praise God in his holiness (?William) | 74v | 77 | 65v | 73v | 61v | 76 | 55v | 69 |
| Wilkinson (Thomas or William) fl.1574 - 96 | | | | | | | | |
| Hear my prayer, O Lord, and let thine ear | 97 | 83 | 82v | | | 81v | | |
| O Jerusalem, thou that killest the prophets | 67v | 69v | 59v | 66 | 59 | 70v | 58v | 49 |
| Preserve me, O Lord | 97v<br>98v | | 82 | | | | | |
| Why art thou so full of heaviness? | 67v | 69v | 59v | 66v | 59 | 70v<br>72 | 58v | 49 |
| Wise (Michael) c1648 - 1687 | | | | | | | | |
| Morning and Evening Service in D minor | 51v | 41v | 45v | 39v | 47 | 52v | 46 | 42v |
| Communion Service in D minor | 56v | 57 | 102v | 44 | 51v | 57 | 49 | 46v |
| Communion Service in E | 57 | 46 | 102v | 44 | 51v | | | |
| Awake, put on thy strength | 113 | 108 | 101v | 108v | | | | |
| Awake up my glory | 104v | 94v | 88v | 88 | | | | |
| Blessed is he that considereth the poor | 107v | 97 | 91 | 80 | 73 | | | |

| | Decani | | | | Cantoris | | | |
|---|---|---|---|---|---|---|---|---|
| | M | C-t | T | B | M | C-t | T | B |
| Blessed is the man (Ps. 1) | 102v | 93 | 86 | 86v | 70v | 87 | 67 | 72v |
| By the waters of Babylon | 107 | 96v | 90v | 90 | 72v | | | |
| Have pity on me | 71 | 73v | | | 84 | | 80 | 83v |
| How are the mighty fallen | 105 | 95v | 89 | 88v | | | | 69 |
| I will sing a new song | 81v | | | | | 67 | 82v | 66v |
| O praise God in his holiness | 78 | 108v | | 69 | | | 83v | |
| Prepare ye the way | 77v | 108v | | 109 | | | 83 | |
| The Lord said unto my Lord | 79 | 57v | | 69v | | | 84 | |

## Appendix I

### The Westminster Abbey-Tucker-Bing connection.

As noted in the Introduction (p.6 supra), Bing was paid for copying music for Westminster Abbey in the 1670's. Furthermore, his own set of part-books now at York include such annotations as 'as its in Mr Tucker's Books' and 'as its in ye West (Westminster) Books'. William Tucker, Minor Canon of Westminster Abbey and Gentleman of the Chapel Royal, who died in February 1678/9, did a good deal of music copying both for the Abbey and for the Chapel Royal;[1] and if Bing's further notes such as 'in ye Ch Books' and 'ye K Books' do in fact refer to the 'Chapel' and to the 'King's' Books, it may well have been through his Abbey colleague Tucker that he obtained sight of these.

Survivals of Tucker's Chapel Royal work are available as follows:

(a) The Chapel part-books now in the Music Room of the British Library (Reference Division), RM 27.a.1-6.[2]

(b) A single Bass part-book, now Add.MS 50860 in the British Library (Reference Division).

(c) A single Bass chorus part-book now in the Nanki Music Library, Tokyo, Call No.N-5/10.

(d) Portions of an Organ book now in the Fitzwilliam Museum, Cambridge (Music Mss 152).[3]

Of these (b) and (c), though differing in format (the one upright folio, the other smaller oblong) may well be connected with the set of 'Anthems with Symphonies' mentioned in footnote 1, page 94. A repertory of anthems of that character having no relevance for Bing, the contents of these two MSS are not of interest strictly for present purposes. (Nanki N-5/10 contains a few non-'Symphony' anthems added after the portion copied by Tucker.) However, information about them not being readily accessible, a summary account is given in Appendix III infra. As to (a), the following Services and anthems are still to be found in the Chapel Royal Books RM27.a.1-6 on pages in Tucker's hand surviving from what must have been many more written by him but now perished. Everything except Purcell's 'Lord, who can tell?' is found in Bing's books.

| | |
|---|---|
| Aldrich | Service in E minor |
| | Service in G |
| Amner | O come hither (ending) |
| Blow | Service in G |
| | O God, wherefore art thou absent? |
| | O how amiable are thy dwellings |
| | O Lord, thou hast searched me out |
| | Save me, O God (Ps. 69) |
| | The Lord hear thee |
| Child | Service in A minor |
| | Service in E minor (incomplete) |
| | O Lord, rebuke me not |
| Humfrey | Haste thee, O God |
| | Hear, O heavens |
| | Like as the hart |
| | Lord, teach us to number |
| Locke | Lord, let me know mine end |
| Purcell | Lord, who can tell how oft |
| Tucker | O give thanks (Ps. 107) |
| Turner | Lord, thou hast been our refuge |
| Wise | Awake, put on thy strength |

A more copious repertory on Tucker's hand is still extant in two part-books at Westminster Abbey, Alto Cantoris 'No 1A' and Tenor Cantoris 'No 4', which correspond to each other in their contents.[4] It will readily be observed how much of this is to be found in Bing's set at York: only Aldrich's 'If the Lord himself' and Blow's 8-part 'God is our hope' are not common to both.

| | |
|---|---|
| Aldrich | Service in G |
| | If the Lord himself |
| Batten | Let my complaint |
| Blow | Service in E minor |
| | Service in G |
| | Behold, how good and joyful |
| | Christ rising again |
| | Lord, how are they increased |
| | God is our hope and strength (a 8) |
| | O how amiable are thy dwellings |
| | O God, wherefore art thou absent? |
| | O Lord, I have sinned |
| | O Lord, thou hast searched me out |
| | Save me, O God (Ps.69) |
| | Sing we merrily |
| | The Lord hear thee |
| | Turn thee unto me |

| | |
|---|---|
| Child | Service in A minor |
| | Service in E minor |
| | 'Flat Service in E' |
| | Behold, how good and joyful |
| | O Lord, rebuke me not |
| | The earth is the Lord's |
| | Thou art my king, O God |
| Ferrabosco | Evening Service |
| C.Gibbons | The Lord said unto my Lord |
| Humfrey | Service in E minor |
| | By the waters of Babylon |
| | Haste thee, O God |
| | Hear, O heavens |
| | Like as the hart |
| | Lord, teach us to number our days |
| | O be joyful in the Lord |
| | O give thanks (Ps.118) |
| | O Lord my God |
| | Rejoice in the Lord, O ye righteous |
| W.Lawes | Let God arise |
| Locke | Not unto us |
| Purcell | Blessed be the Lord my strength |
| | Blow up the trumpet |
| | I will sing unto the Lord |
| | Let God arise |
| | O God, the king of glory |
| | O Lord our governor |
| Rogers | I beheld, and lo! a great multitude |
| | O clap your hands |
| Tucker | Benedicite Service |
| | Evening Service |
| | Comfort ye |
| | I am well pleased |
| | I was glad |
| | I will magnify thee |
| | Lord, how long wilt thou be angry? |
| | My heart is fixed |
| | O clap your hands |
| | O give thanks (Ps.105) |
| | This is the day |
| | Wherewithal shall a young man |
| Tudway | Behold, God is my salvation |
| Turner | Lord, thou hast been our refuge |
| Wise | Awake up, my glory |
| | How are the mighty fallen |
| | O praise God in his holiness |
| Humfrey Turner & Blow | I will alway give thanks |

It should be said that though the musical notation of these works is in Tucker's hand, he employed assistants to help with the verbal text. What is a particularly interesting feature from the present point of view is that at the front of both books a separate single leaf has been inserted before what was originally the first item, Blow's Benedicite Service. Each of these single leaves carries 'Dr Blow's Te Deum to his Benedicite Service' and is in the hand not of Tucker but of Bing (in the style of Plate II), who must have added this between the date of Blow's doctorate (December 1677) and his own death. Again, following the last item transcribed by Tucker in each book (Thomas Tomkins's 'Let my complaint'), Bing takes up his pen and adds 'Dr Blow's Kyrie & Creed to his Service in Gamut' on the next pages.

All subsequent items is these books are post-Tucker/Bing, but Bing himself makes an interesting appearance in a third Westminster part-book, Tenor Decani '5'. This is now a composite volume into which, for economy's sake four groups of older leaves from some earlier were built. These four groups, which are not contiguous to each other, contain the following items by Bing (also in the style of Plate II) in the order here shown:

| | | |
|---|---|---|
| A. | Thomas Tomkins | *Second Service (beginning in the middle of 8) |
| | Portman | *Service in G (2,4,6,7,8,10) |
| | Bryne | *Service in G (2,5,6,7,8,10) |
| | Rogers | *Behold, now praise the Lord |
| | Child | *Service in D (2,5,6,7,8,10) |
| | | *Service in F (2,5,6,7,9,11) |
| | | *'Benedicite' Service in G (3,5,6,7,8,10,2) |
| B. | Patrick | *Service in G minor (part of 2,4,6,7,part of 8) |
| | Blow | *Service in A (part of 2,5,6,7,9,11) |
| | Orlando Gibbons | +Second Service (8,10) |
| C. | Tye | *+(Ending of) I will exalt thee (with 2nd part, Sing unto the Lord) |
| | William Mundy | *+O Lord, the maker of all thing |
| | William Mundy | *+O Lord, the world's saviour |
| | Hooper | *+Teach me thy way |
| | Orlando Gibbons | *+Almighty and everlasting God |
| | Batten | *+O praise the Lord, all ye heathen |
| | | *+Haste thee, O God (with 2nd part) |
| | | *+When the Lord turned again the captivity |
| | | *Deliver us, O Lord our God |
| | | *My soul truly waiteth |

This sequence in the York books

| | | | |
|---|---|---|---|
| | Child | | *Praise the Lord, O my soul (Ps.103) |
| | | | *O Lord, grant the king a long life |
| | | | *If the Lord himself |
| | Batten | | Sing joyfully |
| | Child | | *O pray for the peace of Jerusalem |
| | Rogers | | *Teach me, O Lord |
| D. | Tallis | This sequence in the York books | *+With all our hearts |
| | Hooper | | *+Blessed be thy name, O God |
| | William Mundy | | *+O thou God, Almighty Father |
| | Tallis | | *+O Lord, I bow the knees |
| | Byrd | | *+I call and cry |
| | Hooper | | *+Prevent us, O Lord |
| | | | *+Behold, it is Christ |

This sequence in Barnard

*In Bing's hand in the books now at York

+In Barnard's First Book of Selected Church Musick (1641)

## References to Appendix I

1. WAM 33712. 1677: 'To Mr Tucker for Coppying out some Musick bookes for the use of the Church xl'; 'To him more on the like Occassion xl.' £20 must have represented a considerable amount of work, going back probably more than one year. At the time of his death a sum of £15 was owing to him for 'writing in 15 books the Anthems with Symphonies for King Charles the 2nds use in his Chappell Royal'. See J.Y.Akerman, Moneys. . .for Secret Service of Charles II and James II (Camden Society, London, 1851), p.98.

2. These, formerly RM 23.m.1-6, were discussed by me in 'A Contemporary Source of English Music of the Purcellian Period', Acta Musicologica, vol.31 (1959), pp.38-44. I subsequently identified Tucker as the scribe of the items which I there listed from 'the first group of older leaves'. A further nine books have come to light recently so that the whole set is now collectively known as RM 27.a.1-15, but only the first six books preserve a record of Tucker's activity.

3. See my paper, 'A Cambridge Manuscript from the English Chapel Royal', Music & Letters, vol.42 (1961), pp.263-7.

4. It is very possible that these books were among those at Westminster Abbey known to Vincent Novello long ago but thereafter overlooked until Dr Douglas Guest found them among choir music and passed them to the Abbey Library. See The Cathedral Service, Anthems. . . by Henry Purcell, edited by Vincent Novello, 4 vols, London, 1828.

## Appendix II

### The St Paul's Cathedral-Bing-Gostling connection

Six part-books survive at St Paul's Cathedral containing material copied c1675-c1700. Two of them (Contratenor and Tenor Decani) are devoted to Services, the others (Contratenor, Tenor, and Bass Decani; Bass Cantoris) to Anthems.

The two books of Services are very largely in the hand of Bing of the character of Plate II, but one or two pages are missing, and one or two others, inserted no doubt to make good some damaged passages, are in a much later hand. The repertory of the Bing sections of both books, which may be compared with that of the York books, is as follows:

| | |
|---|---|
| Aldrich | E minor (Benedicite Service) |
| | G |
| Batten | Short |
| Bevin | Short |
| Bryne | Short |
| Blow | A |
| | E minor (Benedicite Service) |
| Byrd | Short |
| Child | A minor |
| | E minor |
| | 'Flat Service in E' |
| | F |
| | G (Benedicite Service) |
| | Verse Evening Service in G |
| Farrant (J.) | Short |
| Farrant (R.) | 'High' |
| Gibbons (O.) | Short |
| Humfrey | E minor |
| Patrick | G minor |
| Portman | G |
| Rogers | E minor (Verse) |
| | D |
| | G |
| Tomkins (T.) | C |
| | D minor (Second Service) |
| Tucker | F (Benedicite Service) |

It appears that at the point when he reached the two Services of Aldrich and that by Tucker, Bing had come to the end of his time. In the Tenor Decani book all three are in his writing, Aldrich being designated 'Mr', as indeed he was up to Bing's death. But some slight change of hand can be discerned in these works in the Contratenor book, and this appears on inspection to be that of John Gostling endeavouring to match Bing's style as much as possible, in particular in the downward stems of the notes and the avoidance of the typically Gostling backward-looped 'd'. Moreover, in this book Aldrich appears as 'Dr', a status he acquired on 2 March 1681/2, that is to say after Bing's death. In due course the characteristically personal hand of Gostling asserts itself. His contribution to these books is therefore:

| | |
|---|---|
| Aldrich | in E minor (Contratenor only) |
| | G (Contratenor only) |
| Blow | E minor (Contratenor only) |
| Purcell | B flat |
| Rogers | A minor |
| Wise | D minor (Contratenor only) |

The four anthem books as they now stand are 'cannibalised'; that is to say when they were constituted in the 18th century substantial sections from earlier books were built into them. Those earlier sections, which may be differentiated from the later at a mere glance, are in John Gostling's hand, long stretches being in that style, as noticed in the Service books, accommodating itself to Bing's but giving place eventually to his personal manner. The repertory of those sections is rather too extensive, even if relevant, to be set out here, but in summary it is closely on the lines of Bing's anthology (from which much of the text may indeed have been derived), with a few later works by Blow and Purcell added.

It stops short of anything of the Clarke and Croft generation. Quite early in the Full Anthem part of the Contratenor Decani book there is Byrd's 'O Lord, make thy servant William, our king', which could not have been entered at the earliest before 1688 and more probably not until 1694 or after; and no more than some ten items further on we reach Blow's 'My God, my God, look upon me' which was not composed until

6 September, 1697. One therefore judges that this extensive amount of copying by Gostling represents concentrated work in the period 1695-1700 when the reconstituted choir of the Cathedral once more became fully active, more particularly after the opening of the Choir of Wren's building in 1697.

## Appendix III

### Chapel Royal Part-books of 'Anthems with Symphonies' in the hand of William Tucker (February 1678/9)

(A) British Museum (Reference Division), Add. MS 50860. Bass part. Upright folio with royal arms on front cover and what appears to be the youthful signature of W.Crofts (sic) with date 1697 inside back cover. Formerly belonging to Richard Border and W.H.Cummings. In three items Tucker has employed an assistant to help with the verbal text. Some pages of the book are now missing.

(B) Nanki Library, Tokyo, N-5/10. Bass chorus part. Small oblong. Formerly belonging to W.H.Cummings and E.J.Hopkins. The book has been scrawled upon by (apparently) Chapel Royal choristers, among them Edmund Baker, later organist of Chester Cathedral, whose voice had changed by 28 December 1710. In several places Tucker has employed an assistant to help with the verbal text, one of them being the same as in (A) above. This book has extensive additions made after Tucker's work, and some pages are now missing. In the list below, only items with which Tucker had to do are mentioned.

An intriguing feature of (B) is the endorsement on the page devoted to the 'Club' Anthem:

Compos'd by Pell; Humfrey. Will: Turner. John Blow

The two last names are certainly in the form of autograph signatures of the two composers, and the words 'Compos'd by Pell: Humfrey' may possibly be in Humfrey's writing. If so, the endorsement must date from between about mid-April 1674 and his death (having made his Will on 23 April) on 14 July of that year, because only five pages earlier occurs Blow's 'When Israel came out of Egypt', which was composed on 5 April 1674 (Bodleian Library, MS Mus. Sch. c.39, p.112 and c.58, f.9v).

| | | | |
|---|---|---|---|
| Blow | And I heard a great voice | A | B |
| | Arise, O Lord | | B |
| | I beheld, and lo! a great multitude | A | B |
| | Sing we merrily | | B |
| | the kings of Tharsis | | B |
| | The Lord is my shepherd | A | B |
| | When Israel came out of Egypt | A | B |
| | When the Lord turned again | A | |
| Humfrey | By the waters of Babylon | A | B |
| | Haste thee, O God | A | B |
| | Hear my crying | A | B |
| | O be joyful | A | |
| | O give thanks (Ps.118) | A | B |
| | O praise the Lord, laud ye | A | |
| | Rejoice in the Lord, O ye righteous | A | B |
| | The king shall rejoice | | B |
| | Thou art my king, O God | A | B |
| Humfrey<br>Turner<br>Blow | I will alway give thanks | | B |
| Locke | God is gone up | A | B |
| | God reigneth | | B |
| | O clap your hands together | A | B |
| Purcell | If the Lord himself | A | B |
| | My beloved spake | A | |
| | Praise the Lord, ye servants | A | B |
| Tudway | O come let us sing unto the Lord | A | |
| Turner | Hold not thy tongue, O God | | B |
| | O praise the Lord (Psalm 147) | A | B |